"This practical resour[c]e ... sound theological fram[e] ... with an emphasis on app[ly] ... must-read for Sunday school teachers and parents ...."

Marty Machowski, Family Pastor; author of *The Ology, Long Story Short, The Gospel Story Bible,* and other gospel-centered resources for church and home

"*How to Teach Kids Theology* will help you capture a biblical vision and the practical tools to encourage children to develop a deep and robust faith in Christ. This book is a valuable resource to help you focus on what matters most in ministry to children."

Josh Mulvihill, Executive Director of Church and Family Ministry, Renewanation; author of *50 Things Every Child Needs to Know Before Leaving Home*

"More than ever, our kids must not only know the Word of God but have the tools to properly apply it in everyday life. *How to Teach Kids Theology* is a must-have guide for anyone who influences the next generation and wants to see our kids have a greater understanding of theology."

Steven J. Adams, Executive Director, International Network of Children's Ministry

"There are plenty of books on theology and plenty of books on how to teach kids, but far too few books on how to teach kids theology. Sam and Hunter provide an important resource to help fill this void. Practical, accessible, and weighty, *How to Teach Kids Theology* will be a great help to the church and home."

Brian Dembowczyk, Author of *Gospel Centered Kids Ministry* and *Family Discipleship That Works*

"This book is much more than a how-to guide. It's also rocket fuel. It will get you fired up about the unsearchable riches of Christ and eager to help kids see every angle of his splendor. If you teach the Bible and want to do it even better in ways that wow your students with Jesus, read this book."

Jack Klumpenhower, Author of *Show Them Jesus*

"In *How to Teach Kids Theology*, Sam and Hunter provide a vital resource for ministry leaders and parents, offering practical tools to build a solid foundation of faith in the next generation. This book not only makes those timeless truths accessible but also transforms how children understand and navigate the world around them."

Andy Kirk, OneHope Global Kids Ministry Ambassador

"This book provides such great insight and helps to reorient our thinking around our first ministry: our own children. The helpful illustrations, big-picture mapping, and sample lessons will give you a game plan to be an effective teacher to your kids. It is a must-read for the church today!"

Nate Sala, Teacher; speaker; president of Wise Disciple

"This book is such a gift to those who desperately want help in training their children to know and obey everything Christ commanded. For the parent or ministry leader who is intimidated by theology, Sam and Hunter expertly walk us through both how to think about theology and how to make what we know about God accessible for our whole family."

Adam Griffin, Lead Pastor, Eastside Community Church, Dallas, TX; host of *The Family Discipleship Podcast*; author of several books and resources for families

"Luce and Williams bring the lofty topic of theology down from the top shelf, making it accessible and engaging for all ages. Every teacher and parent will find this book invaluable for those curious questions that arise. With its creative approach, these pages will help you answer tough questions and spark meaningful and lasting conversations. Keep this book close—you'll reach for it often."

Ron Hunter Jr., CEO of D6 Family Ministry; author of several family ministry and leadership books

HOW TO TEACH KIDS THEOLOGY

Deep Truths for Growing Faith

Sam Luce and Hunter Williams

New
Growth
Press

newgrowthpress.com

New Growth Press, Greensboro, NC 27401
newgrowthpress.com

Cover Design: Faceout Books, faceoutstudio.com
Interior Typesetting and eBook: Lisa Parnell, lparnellbookservices.com

ISBN: 978-1-64507-485-4 (paperback)
ISBN: 978-1-64507-486-1 (ebook)

Library of Congress Cataloging-in-Publication Data on file

Names: Luce, Sam, 1975- author. | Williams, Hunter, 1992- author.
Title: How to teach kids theology : deep truths for growing faith / by Sam Luce and Hunter Williams.
Description: Greensboro, NC : New Growth Press, [2024] | Includes bibliographical references. | Summary: "Takes the deep truths of the Christian faith and gives practical, actionable direction for sharing them with children"-- Provided by publisher.
Identifiers: LCCN 2024042735 (print) | LCCN 2024042736 (ebook) | ISBN 9781645074854 (paperback) | ISBN 9781645074861 (ebook)
Subjects: LCSH: Christian education--Teaching methods. | Christian education of children.
Classification: LCC BV1475.3 .L83 2024 (print) | LCC BV1475.3 (ebook) | DDC 268--dc23/eng/20241113
LC record available at https://lccn.loc.gov/2024042735
LC ebook record available at https://lccn.loc.gov/2024042736

Printed in the United States of America

29 28 27 26 25   2 3 4 5 6

To my mom and dad, Paul and Annie Luce, who taught me to treasure Christ and trust him above all else. They were also the first children's pastors I ever knew. Much of what I have written here started as seeds they faithfully planted in me.

– Sam Luce

To my wife, Sammie, and our four children—Margot, Clarke, Opal, and Joy—whose love and lives are undeserved gifts I cherish with all my heart. To my parents, Ray and Tina Williams, who faithfully raised me in the love and admonition of the Lord, and to all the leaders who declared and displayed the truths of God's Word throughout my life. Your investments are on full display in these pages.

– Hunter Williams

Contents

Lack of Confidence = Lots of Confusion

I (Hunter) find research books to be both fascinating and infuriating. My reactions can rapidly swing between comfort and concern, and I felt both in abundance while reading *Children's Ministry in a New Reality* by the Barna Research Group. I received a copy the day it was released and was ready to uncover the research. When the book arrived in the mail, I immediately ripped open the packaging, sat on my couch, and began wading through the data with a highlighter in hand.

CONFUSION

I planned to read the book quickly and then go back to slowly digest the insights I had highlighted. This plan worked until I got to chapter 2. One statistic stopped me dead in my tracks. Barna asked respondents to measure their comfort level for leading children in conversations about various spiritual topics. Of all the options given, children's ministry leaders marked that they were the most uncomfortable in leading conversations about major doctrines of the church.[1]

I was confused. You think this would be the topic with which leaders would be the most comfortable, but close to 40 percent stated otherwise. The follow-up question made this fact even more shocking. Children's ministry leaders were asked to rate their comfort level with leading conversations about social topics, and respondents shared that they were more comfortable discussing topics such as technology and culture than they were about doctrines of the church.[2] My confusion turned into concern when I paired this lack of confidence with the decline and departure of young people from the church.

According to a few in-depth studies released by the Barna Group, approximately 64 percent of students had dropped out of church at some point during their twenties.[3] Lifeway produced a similar study showing that 66 percent of teenagers who attended church regularly in high school dropped out for at least a year after graduation.[4] Combined, these studies show that around two-thirds of church-attending children disengage from the church after high school, with some never returning. Why?

One study from the Barna Group states that 23 percent of teenagers left the church because the Bible was not taught clearly or often enough.[5] Likewise, Lifeway's Research shows that 16 percent of those who stopped attending church did so because the church was not helping them develop spiritually. These statistics reveal the sad reality that some children grow up and leave the church as young adults because they've been presented with a lackluster view of God that has no bearing on their lives. He is seen as a good idea that turns into an irrelevant memory once they are grown and experience the harsh realities of life.

Growing in Confidence

How can the church change the tide? If it's true that ministry leaders and parents struggle to pass on primary doctrines of the faith due to lack of training, then churches should make such instruction a top priority. Training and tools are needed to equip members and families to study Scripture competently and teach its truths confidently, but what resources exist to make this a reality?

> There are wonderful books that tell readers *what to say* about theological topics, but few teach readers *how to think about what they say* when teaching kids theology.

Books such as *The Ology* and *Big Truths for Young Hearts* are wonderful gifts to the church that provide great scripts and stories for parents to read to their kids about theology, but they don't teach readers how to uncover and deliver these truths for themselves. The church needs books that provide leaders with the principles and practices needed to teach biblical passages and stories to kids with theological conviction and competency. Our prayer is that this book does just that.

LAY OF THE LAND

With a title like *How to Teach Kids Theology*, you might approach this book with several expectations. You might be expecting complete lesson plans, classroom management techniques, or expositions on every core doctrine of Christianity. To ensure you start with the right expectations, we want to provide a "lay of the land."

Each chapter is divided into three sections: the problem, the principle, and the practice. In each chapter, we diagnose a problem that hinders leaders from teaching theology to kids, explain the principle that combats the problem, and then suggest practices for applying the principle to your ministry. Along with these sections, each chapter concludes with discussion questions that help leaders and parents reinforce what they've read and, more specifically, apply it to their contexts.

Since we're teaching you how to think about what you teach, the first three chapters lay a foundation for the need, nature, and scope of theology. Chapter 1 discusses the problem of distorted views of God and how teaching theology well tackles this issue. Chapter 2 defines theology and explains why every leader is called to teach it, and chapter 3 speaks to the practical nature of theology and its impact on every sphere of life. While several examples and practices are given in these early chapters, the practices increase exponentially as the book progresses.

After the foundation has been laid, chapters 4–6 apply the framework from the early chapters to specific aspects of teaching. Since accurate Bible study is essential to sound theology, chapter 4 teaches leaders how to read, study, and apply Scripture through a gospel-centered lens. Chapter 5 helps leaders understand the difference between watering down the truth and teaching it in age-appropriate ways, while chapter 6 focuses on cultivating theological charity as we strive toward theological clarity.

Because the book progresses in its application of the principles, chapters 7–8 end on a practical high note. Chapter 7 discusses specific tools and helps readers develop a clearly defined "pathway" for teaching theology to kids as they grow, while chapter 8 equips leaders and parents for theological formation in the home. The book wraps up with a conclusion and a few appendices that further aid readers in their role of teaching theology.

We pray this book will equip you to fulfill the Great Commission and teach kids theology with greater confidence in the classroom and at home.

Let's get started!

Chapter 1

Seeing the Great Lion: Why We Need to Teach Kids Theology

The question shot out like a rocket and filled our classroom with silence. I (Hunter) had just finished teaching a Bible lesson in our children's ministry and was asked to facilitate a small group of fourth and fifth graders. Since I didn't normally lead this group, I spent most of the time getting to know the kids and opened the floor for questions. Immediately, one boy (we'll call him Austin) asked, "Could Satan defeat Jesus?"

Our lesson that morning was on the ascension of Jesus and how he is both defending and preparing a place for those who believe in him (John 14:1–3). When I asked the group if they had any questions, I expected to receive inquiries about the return of Christ, my favorite sports team, or what heaven might look like. Instead, I got multiple questions on the power of Satan and whether he could foil Jesus's plans.

After answering a few questions, I discovered the problem. The issue wasn't Austin's big view of Satan but his small view of God. He feared the schemes of Satan *more* than the ascending power of Jesus. He thought the King of heaven could be outwitted by the Father of Lies and the Prince of Peace could be overcome by the Prince of Darkness. His evaluation of the devil was overrated because his appreciation of God was underdeveloped.

If Austin didn't come to see Jesus as the conquering Lion of Judah, he would never see the devil as the scaredy-cat that he is. Austin needed to know God, and it was my responsibility to help him see God clearly.

THE PROBLEM: DISTORTED VISIONS OF GOD

A. W. Tozer famously said, "What comes into our minds when we think about God is the most important thing about us."[1] If this is true (and we think it is), then teaching about God is our most important task. This can't be overstated!

The God of the universe has entrusted us with the life-changing message of the gospel and commissioned us to make disciples of the children in our care (Matthew 28:19–20). This is no small calling. We've been charged to form our children into the likeness of Christ (Romans 8:29) and to help them become like the Savior they follow. Since our children can't see Jesus, they will form themselves into the image we paint of him, and if we present a blurry picture of Christ, their discipleship will reflect it.

Sunday school teachers, parents, and ministry leaders must work together to paint an accurate portrait of Christ, not a caricature of him. Caricatures overemphasize certain features of a person to the point of distortion. Their eyes are exaggerated, or their heads are drawn out of proportion to their bodies. We can do the same to Jesus. If we're not careful, we can exaggerate his friendship to the neglect of his lordship or overly emphasize his love to the detriment of his holiness. Conversely, we can magnify Christ's holiness to the denigration of his mercy and grace. One caricature paints Christ as a compliant chum, while the other portrays him as a mean-spirited killjoy.

Children are often presented with caricatures of God because of their age and stage of development. It's assumed that they can't comprehend the deeper truths of the Christian faith, so God is explained in simplified, watered-down language. The problem with these accommodations is that they lend themselves to methods of teaching that minimize God's character and works.

When children are given a minimized understanding of God, it distorts their view of him, which can have a myriad of adverse effects. It can dilute their worship, downplay their commitment to Christ's mission, and disconnect their lives from his truth. Children cannot live beyond their perception of God; if their perception of him is misguided, their lives will be misdirected. This is why passivity isn't an option. If we aren't deliberate in developing our children's understanding of God, then it will be developed by someone else.

In our individualistic society, kids can get the impression that God is just a means of guaranteeing their personal happiness. In fact, one of the prevailing views of God in America is found within a belief system known as "Moralistic Therapeutic Deism."[2] In this view, God is seen as a distant deity that intervenes in people's lives to help them do good and feel good. It's a mix of vague religious concepts and individualistic thinking that turns God into a cosmic pushover whose concerns are limited to the behaviors of people.

It's similar to the genie found in Aladdin's lamp. He's a powerful being tucked away in a golden lamp who is summoned by individuals who say the right words, follow the rules, and make their wishes known. In like manner, the god of this counterfeit religion is a powerful being that is kept away in heaven only to be summoned by the concerns of individuals who play nice, keep the rules, and make their desires known. Not only does this belief system belittle God and reduce him to the status of a divine butler, but it trivializes humanity's sin and strips the cross of its power.

Sadly, this contorted view of God dominates our culture and many of our churches, making it difficult for children to know God truly and follow him faithfully. If we want our kids to see God as the "Great I Am" and not merely as the "good that was," then our teaching needs to reflect the awe-inspiring, life-altering, heart-transforming greatness of God and the goodness of his gospel. Their spiritual growth requires it, and their resolve to his cause is built on it.

THE PRINCIPLE: CLEAR VISIONS OF GOD CHANGE EVERYTHING

In C. S. Lewis's *The Lion, the Witch, and the Wardrobe*, the Pevensie children (Peter, Susan, Edmund, and Lucy) went through a wooden wardrobe that transported them to the magical world of Narnia. Once there, they encountered talking beasts and an evil white witch who had cursed Narnia with an eternal winter. They soon discovered that the only one who could save the realm of Narnia from the bitter curse was the great lion, Aslan. Through his sacrificial death, resurrection, and power, Aslan defeated the evil witch and brought new life to Narnia.

Later, in *Prince Caspian*, the children were summoned back to Narnia by a bewildered prince who needed help. Along the way, Lucy, the youngest of the children, caught glimpses of Aslan, but the others didn't believe her when she told them. While everyone is asleep, Lucy entered the woods and saw Aslan. Once they finished their warm welcome, Lucy gazed into Aslan's eyes and said,

> "Aslan, you're bigger."
> "That is because you are older, little one," answered he.
> "Not because you are?"
> "I am not. But every year you grow older, you will find me bigger."[3]

I recently reread this conversation between Aslan and Lucy, and it gave me chills. It's a beautiful picture of what the Christian life is supposed to look like and a powerful reminder of what our children should experience in their relationships with Christ. Aslan, who was reminiscent of Jesus, didn't change throughout the course of the series. He hadn't grown in size or increased in power. It's Lucy who had changed. She had grown in her understanding of Aslan, which made him appear bigger in her eyes.

Our children should undergo this same kind of growth in their experience with God. In Christ, "there is no variation or shadow due to change" (James 1:17). He doesn't grow in wisdom, and he doesn't increase in power. It is our children's love for God that grows and their understanding of him that expands. With every step our children take in their Christian walks, God should grow bigger in their eyes. Their awe of his greatness should gradually increase, and their commitment to his cause should continually deepen.

Lionlike resolve

Lucy's perception of Aslan isn't the only thing that changed. The course of her life changed as well. Aslan commanded Lucy to wake the others and follow him, but they couldn't see him. Lucy was deemed to be crazy but follows Aslan wherever he leads despite the cynical remarks of her siblings and allies. She chose to follow Aslan in the face of mockery and skepticism because he was worth it.

Lucy would have had difficulty trusting Aslan and taking his words seriously if he were a mere kitten. She had great commitment because the one she was committed to was great. Not only was Aslan a powerful lion worth trusting, but he empowered Lucy with the clarity and strength she needed to follow him faithfully. He was both the object of her commitment and the source of her courage.

If we want our kids to stand firm in a culture that suppresses the truth of Christianity, we need to give them a grand view of God that overwhelms their hearts and fills them with wonder. Our children's resolve is only as strong as the God they believe in, and if the God they believe in is presented to them as nothing more than a small deity, their loyalty will follow suit.

> We can't teach kids kitty-cat theology and expect them to have lion-like resolve.

For their resolve to be great, they will need to be shown a God that is great. This comes by teaching good theology to kids—a knowledge of God that is true.

The greatest gift

Again, teaching our children about God is our most important task. It's also the greatest gift we give. A. W. Tozer said: "We do the greatest service to the next generation of Christians by passing on to them undimmed and undiminished that noble concept of God which we received from our Hebrew and Christian fathers of generations past. This will prove of greater value to them than anything that art or science can devise."[4]

Churches can provide children with dynamic ministry experiences full of fun activities, engaging worship music, and meaningful relationships. However, if these things aren't grounded in the "undiminished concept of God" revealed in the person of Christ and his Word, then they become cheap gifts void of power.

Children can experience fun activities at local clubs and sports teams. They can engage in dynamic music at concerts and music camps and build meaningful relationships in their neighborhoods and schools. The one thing these people and places cannot offer them is the good news of the gospel. They cannot direct their hearts to worship the eternal, immortal, and only wise God (1 Timothy 1:17 KJV). They cannot cultivate fellowship in the unity of the Spirit, and they cannot nourish their souls.

If we want what's best for our kids, we will put our time and energy into what matters most: the glory of God. The act of making much of God and pleasing him in our ministries starts by taking our call to teach seriously. We dishonor God when we wing it or flippantly handle his Word. Every time we teach, we tell our kids, "This is what God is like." We must ensure that what we say about God is accurate and true. Otherwise, we're teaching a false god.

I'm not trying to elicit fear or limit children's ministry to experts. As we'll see in chapter 2, we all teach something about God, whether we realize it or not. My intent is to show the weight of our calling. When we downplay the importance of teaching theology to kids because "they're just kids," we're basically telling God that the importance of his commission and glory depends on the age and location of those we serve. When we keep God's glory and his Great Commission at the forefront, this focus keeps our hearts in check and informs what and how we teach.

THE PRACTICE: RELENTLESSLY FOCUS ON GOD

When Austin asked, "Can Jesus lose?" merely saying no wouldn't have sufficed. He needed to know why Jesus couldn't lose, and the answer is found in who Jesus is. I told Austin that we know that Satan could never triumph because Jesus already has. Colossians 2:14–15 tells us that because of Christ's death on the cross, he has humiliated the rulers of darkness by triumphing over them. This is why Jesus came! He became a man, died, rose, and ascended to heaven "to destroy the works of the devil" (1 John 3:8). Jesus is our conquering King who defeated death to destroy the power of Satan and secure our freedom (Hebrews 2:14–15).

Not only is Jesus the one who conquers on our behalf, but he is the creator of all things. Colossians 1:16 says, "For by him all things were created, in heaven and on earth, visible and invisible, whether thrones or dominions or rulers or authorities—all things were created through him and for him." This includes Satan. Since Jesus created Satan, Jesus controls Satan. Satan might be described as a prowling lion, but he's on a very tight leash (1 Peter 5:8). His very existence is held in Christ's hands (Colossians 1:17). Of course, this led to more questions: "Why does Jesus keep Satan alive? He's a bad guy, right? Why doesn't Jesus get rid of him and the demons?"

These are tough questions. It's easy to get defensive or dismissive concerning questions about God, evil, and suffering. One option is to make educated guesses about the intent behind evil acts and events, but I would advise against this. We typically don't know the specific reasons behind such actions. Guessing puts words in God's mouth, and we never want to presume about God's intentions. The other option is to focus on what we know about God and allow that to frame our understanding of evil and suffering. The book of Job provides invaluable insight into this idea.

Show them God's glory

Job is a man who loves God and is blessed with a great family and wealth. Unbeknownst to Job, an accuser approaches God in heaven with a plan to devastate his life and make him curse God. God allows this, and Job suffers greatly. He loses his children and his health. Job's friends visit him and spend most of the book arguing their perspective on his suffering. They assume God's motivations and claim Job is experiencing hardship as punishment for sin in his life.

Job protests and demands an explanation from God. In his grace, God gives Job an answer, but it's not the answer we might expect. Instead of telling Job *why* he suffered, God describes *who* he is. He takes Job on a tour of the universe and details the complexities of his creative acts. When God finishes speaking, Job gives this profound reply:

> "I know that you can do all things,
>   and that no purpose of yours can be thwarted.
> 'Who is this that hides counsel without knowledge?'
> Therefore I have uttered what I did not understand,
>   things too wonderful for me, which I did not
>   know.
> 'Hear, and I will speak;
>   I will question you, and you make it known to
>   me.'
> I had heard of you by the hearing of the ear,
>   but now my eye sees you;
> therefore I despise myself,
>   and repent in dust and ashes." (Job 42:2–6)

Job doesn't feel cheated by God's explanation. Quite the opposite. He says he has seen God and acknowledges his lack of understanding. Catching a glimpse of the immensity and overwhelming splendor of God's work in the world humbles Job and puts his suffering in perspective. It reassembles his categories and causes him to reevaluate everything in light of God's greatness.

When teaching kids about God, we should never try to make him fit into nice, tidy boxes or overly simplistic categories. Our goal isn't to make God convenient or useful but to see him as he truly is and respond accordingly. I think our culture's hyperfixation on the practical has poorly impacted how we approach Scripture in children's ministry. We immediately look for what's useful. But making the practical primary undercuts God and can distort the meaning of Scripture. It makes him a means to an end and not the end of our means.

God should be the goal and prize of our ministries! Teaching about him should be the most exciting thing we do. Kids can love the activities we create and enjoy the snacks we supply, but they especially should look forward to the times when God is taught. Seeing him should be the most exhilarating thing they experience. For this to be the case, we must relentlessly focus on God in everything we do. Before giving our time to events and other elements of ministry, energy should be poured into the weighty task of displaying God's glory. If kids can leave our classrooms or small groups without having their view of God expanded, we've missed the mark. With every Bible lesson and interaction, God should become bigger in their eyes. That's the goal! Anything less is distortion.

Stabilize your priorities by shifting your prayers

One of the best ways to keep our focus on God is to evaluate our prayers. They reveal our goals, dreams, and deepest desires. With that said, consider your most recent prayers. What filled them? What was their focus? What do they reveal about your sense of identity? What do they uncover about your metrics of success? While there are a multitude of things we could pray for in our ministries, I think the apostle Paul provides an excellent example of the type of prayers we should pray for our leaders, kids, and ourselves:

> For this reason, because I have heard of your faith in the Lord Jesus and your love toward all the saints, I do not cease to give thanks for you, remembering you in my prayers, that the God of our Lord Jesus Christ, the Father of glory, may give you the Spirit of wisdom and of revelation in the knowledge of him,

having the eyes of your hearts enlightened, that you
may know what is the hope to which he has called
you, what are the riches of his glorious inheritance
in the saints, and what is the immeasurable greatness
of his power toward us who believe, according to the
working of his great might. (Ephesians 1:15–19)

When was the last time you prayed that the eyes of your kids'
hearts would be opened and that they would see the immeasurable greatness of God's power toward them? What if
we prayed more prayers like this? What would it do to our
hearts? How might it change the way we teach and disciple
our kids? Shifting the focus of our prayers can stabilize our
priorities by exposing the idols of our hearts and reorienting
our desires toward God.

While we are responsible for teaching our children who
God is and showing them what he is like, we must recognize that their resolve and spiritual resilience aren't completely up to us. They need God's Spirit to empower them
toward faithful obedience (Acts 1:8). He alone has the power
to change hearts and transform lives. Though the Spirit is the
one who opens the eyes of a child's heart, our efforts aren't
pointless. The Spirit works through the faithful teaching of
God's Word. Because of this, we can know that our efforts in
helping kids see the greatness of God aren't in vain (Isaiah
55:10–11).

We may not be able to control what children believe,
but we can control what we teach them. We can deliberately
teach them what is true or casually teach them what is easy.
We can give them a simplistic caricature of God, or we can
give them a realistic picture of who he is. We can introduce
them to a great lion, or we can introduce them to a weak cat.
One might get their attention, but the other will acquire their
allegiance. The difference between the two is found in the
type of theology we teach.

DISCUSSION QUESTIONS

1. Caricatures of Christ are easier to paint than faithful portraits. In what ways have you seen Christ disproportionately taught? How can these caricatures be corrected?

2. Job's friends tried to fit God in a box and assumed his intentions in Job's suffering. In what ways are we in danger of constricting God to overly simplistic categories, and what effects can this have on our kids?

3. The apostle Paul prayed bold, spiritually minded prayers for his church. How might Paul's prayers change the way we pray for our kids, parents, and leaders?

Chapter 2

What Is Theology?

What comes to mind when you hear the word *theology*? Big books? Ivory towers? Stuffy classrooms? Whatever you picture theology to be will determine how you approach it. This is why definitions matter. If we start with a flawed understanding of theology, it will affect our study and practice of it.

Unfortunately, theology isn't a primary topic in many children's ministry books, podcasts, and seminars. Most content or training in the "kidmin" world deals with organizational tactics such as volunteer recruitment, safety procedures, and leadership structures. While these elements are important, they lack power and direction if they are devoid of rich theology. I (Hunter) believe theological discourse is often missing from conversations in children's ministry because the definition supplied to leaders and parents gives the impression that theology isn't for them.

The Problem: Poor Definitions of Theology

If you were to do a quick Google search, the most common definition of theology that would appear is "the study of God." This definition comes from the combination of two Greek words—*theos*, meaning "God," and *ology*, which comes from *logos*, meaning "word" or "study."[1] While "the study of God" isn't a bad definition, it can be misleading. It gives the impression that God can only be known through vigorous study or academic rigor and is only obtained in educational settings. This understanding of theology is why many churchgoers leave it to the "professionals," such as pastors or professors.

This "leave-it-to-the-professionals" mentality creates a dangerous dichotomy that says that ministry can be done without teaching theology. But is this possible? Can Sunday school classes, children's church services, or small group gatherings truly function without presenting theology?

I once was invited to speak at an event for kids and conclude my talk with a gospel presentation. As the coordinator relayed the event's details to me, she said, "We want you to teach an engaging Bible lesson, but we don't want you to teach theology. Just tell a simple Bible story and give a brief gospel message."

I don't think the coordinator realized what she was asking me to do. To teach the Bible and present the gospel, I would have to make statements about who God is and what he's done. That's theology! I would have to make claims about sin and the need for a Savior. That's theology! I would have to proclaim that salvation is found in Jesus Christ alone. That's theology! To avoid teaching theology, I would have either had to decline the invitation to speak or attend the event with tape over my mouth. Divorcing ministry and theology just isn't possible, even if the theology being taught is poor or inaccurate.

We think a more helpful definition of theology is "the application of God's revelation to all of life."[2] We like this definition for two reasons. One, it's broader and doesn't give the impression that a person has to be an expert or elite Christian to be a theologian. As we'll see in the following section, everyone receives revelation from God and has a knowledge of him in some form or fashion. That knowledge might be incomplete or distorted due to sin, but it's nevertheless a knowledge of God.

R. C. Sproul echoes this thought in his book *Knowing Scripture*:

> No Christian can avoid theology. Every Christian is a theologian. Perhaps not a theologian in the technical or professional sense, but a theologian nevertheless. The issue for Christians is not whether we are going to be theologians but whether we are going to be good theologians.[3]

Another reason we like this definition is that it acknowledges the practical nature of theology. As we will see in chapter 3, there is no such thing as impractical theology. God reveals himself to all peoples, and their response to his revelation is their application of it. Whether people study God's Word vigorously, or ignore his design in the world intentionally, they are operating as theologians, because they are taking the knowledge of God they've received and applying it in how they allow it to affect their lives. As teachers and parents, you are called to accurately share God's revelation with your kids and teach them how to faithfully apply it to their lives. Theology is a holistic, ongoing practice in which people receive and respond to God's revelation, meaning that all of us are theologians—you, me, and everyone.

THE PRINCIPLE: EVERYONE IS A THEOLOGIAN

Yes, everyone is a theologian, including nonbelievers. Romans 1:18–20 says that God's eternal power and divine nature are clearly shown and perceived by everyone. Creation declares God's glory to all people in all places (Psalm 19:1–6). *If this is true*, you might be wondering, *then why do people falsely understand God or outright deny him?* The short answer is sin. Romans 1:18 says that people suppress the truth of God in unrighteousness. Sin hardens our hearts and leads us to twist God's truth and ignore it (Ephesians 4:18).

This is why we need the gospel! Christ's death and resurrection not only save us from the penalty of sin but also from its power (Romans 6:5–6). In Christ, we are given new minds, and the Spirit opens our eyes to see God rightly (1 Corinthians 2:9–16). As the Spirit works in our hearts, the knowledge of God we once suppressed rises to the surface and begins to change us from the inside out. The beauty of the gospel is that the knowledge we have of God as his redeemed children isn't merely rational. It's relational! Christians aren't distant spectators with a cold propositional knowledge of God; they are children who know their Father personally and are loved by him extravagantly.

The ecosystem of faith

What is theology? It's the revelation of God. But it's not merely knowledge of him. It's knowledge of God that is applied to all of life. It's knowledge that impacts every aspect of our faith (or at least it should). Otherwise, our faith would be disconnected or imbalanced.

For example, if you try to understand human beings apart from an understanding of God, then your view of humans will either be too high or too low. Understanding God as the Holy Creator puts man in his place as a sinful creature who needs saving. On the flip side, understanding the greatness of God helps us see that humans have unique worth as beings made in his image (Genesis 1:26–27). Apart from God, mankind is either upheld as the god of this world or as nothing more than an intelligent beast. Only an accurate knowledge of God can reveal an accurate picture of man.

As you can see, every aspect of our faith is connected. That's why studying doctrine matters. Doctrine simply means "teaching," and our doctrines feed into each other. You could say that the Christian faith is an ecosystem of doctrines.

Ecosystems surround us. As I write this paragraph, I'm watching the ecosystem of my backyard on full display. Various plants are growing in our yard that serve as food for bugs. These bugs are eaten by birds and rodents that serve as prey for our pet cat. This snapshot of my backyard shows how each living thing provides life to the other. "Every factor of an ecosystem depends on every other factor, either directly or indirectly."[4] This is true of our theology as well.

Theology is an ecosystem of faith in which various doctrines (or teachings) depend on one another. This is why kids' ministry leaders and parents should study systematic theology on some level. Systematic theology seeks to organize the doctrines of the Christian faith in an orderly, topical manner, or as John Frame defines it, "Systematic theology seeks to apply Scripture by asking what the *whole* Bible teaches on any subject."[5]

If you were to open a systematic theology book, you would find it divided into various topics or categories. You would see words like "Soteriology," which is the name given to the theology of salvation. In studying this topic, you would learn what all of Scripture has to say about the salvation of mankind in light of who God is. You would also read about other topics, as demonstrated in the graphic below.

Figure 1. The Ecosystem of Theology

The domino effect

Why would the study of systematic theology benefit parents and volunteers? For one, it can help you retain a consistent theology. Becoming familiar with what Scripture says about different doctrines will help you connect the dots between them. Familiarity with the doctrines in Scripture will not only do this but it can also help prevent confusion on certain doctrines.

Scott R. Swain puts it this way:

Confusion about the relationships between various doctrines inevitably leads to confusion about the doctrines themselves. The supreme relationship that systematic theology considers is the relationship between God and everything else. . . . Within a well-ordered system of theology, each doctrine is not only traced to God as its author and end. Each doctrine is also coordinated with other doctrines.[6]

One of my first ministry jobs was serving as a full-time youth pastor. On the first night of leading our youth group, the church hosted a dinner so that students could connect with church members and each other. After I got a plate of food, I sat at a table with a family that had two sisters in our youth ministry. I immediately sparked a conversation to get to know them.

After some initial small talk, they shared about their experiences at the church and what they had learned about Jesus. As the conversation went on, something felt off. I couldn't put my finger on it, but the way these sisters referred to Jesus didn't seem right. I began shifting the conversation to who Jesus is and who they believed him to be. One question revealed the source of my concern. I asked them, "Do you believe that Jesus is God?" This question slowed down what had been a fast-paced conversation. The sisters gave each other a weird look, then asked me, "What do you mean?" I repeated the question: "You say that you believe in Jesus, but do you believe Jesus is God?" With a contorted expression, one sister replied, "I don't know. I know there's a God and that he sent Jesus to save us, but I thought Jesus was just his son. I know Jesus is good, and loving, and stuff, but I never really thought of him as God."

I was floored. Here were two girls who had spent time in this church and its children's ministry yet were confused about basic truths concerning Jesus's identity and the gospel. What fascinated me the most about this conversation was the inconsistency of their theology. On the one hand, they told me they believed Jesus died to save people from sin, which is true. On the other hand, they thought Jesus was merely a perfect human but not God in the flesh. This is a problem since only God can save us (Jonah 2:9). If Jesus is not fully God and fully man, then he can't be our Savior.[7]

Do you see the problem? The sisters' theology of salvation seemed fine on the surface, but since their theology of Christ was wrong, their theology of salvation was skewed. Doctrines are like dominoes; if one falls, the others are knocked down with it. Studying systematic theology can help us avoid this domino effect and more readily recognize when one of the doctrines in our system is fractured or unstable.

Doctrines also act as dominoes in the way they bump into the experiences of our daily lives. The girls in my youth group didn't outright deny the deity of Christ, but their ignorance of his identity has major implications. Just consider the negative effects their poor understanding of Jesus has on their relationship with him and the comfort they experience.

If Jesus is only divine, then he could not be their Great High Priest who sympathizes with them in their weaknesses (Hebrews 4:15). If he is only human, then he could not promise to be with them at all times and in all places (Matthew 28:20). Only Jesus, the God-man, can bring true comfort and hope! In his humanity, he can meet us in our needs with understanding and compassion. In his divinity, he has the power to work in our lives, along with the wisdom to apply his power perfectly to any situation.

Imagine the overwhelming confidence and hope this can give to our kids! Because Jesus is fully human, he knows what it's like to be a child with all its limitations and frustrations. And as God, he knows how to love them perfectly as their heavenly Father. "Oh, the depth of the riches and wisdom and knowledge of God!" (Romans 11:33). Within the deepest doctrines, we find our greatest hopes.

This is the power of theology! If we want our children to have a knowledge of God that is beautiful, true, and good, then we need to accept our role as theologians. You teach theology! The question is whether or not the theology you teach is good.

THE PRACTICE: TEACH GOOD THEOLOGY

If our children are theologians and we teach them theology, how can we ensure that the theology we teach them is good? Much could be said here, but I think the following definition attributed to Thomas Aquinas can serve as a helpful guide. He said, "Theology is taught by God, teaches of God, and leads to God."[8] Each part of this definition is essential for passing on a knowledge of God that is good and true to our kids.

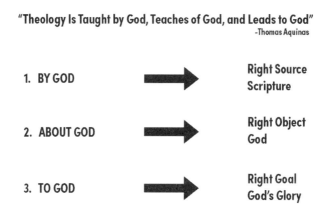

Figure 2. A Framework for Good Theology

Taught *by* God—the right source

Since theology is the revelation of God, there is no one better we can learn theology from than God himself. This might sound obvious, but we have to remember that our children's theology is being shaped on a moment-by-moment basis. Concepts about God might be explicitly taught to them during church services or family devotions, but their perception of God is also being shaped implicitly through conversations, friendships, and social media influencers.[9] In order for our kids to have an accurate knowledge of God, it has to come from the right source—God himself.

God is the only one who knows and reveals himself perfectly. In fact, nothing could be truly known about God unless he revealed himself (Matthew 11:25–27). But how does he do this? What does it look like to be "taught by God"?

As mentioned earlier, God reveals certain aspects of his character and nature through creation (Romans 1:20). He also does this through the inner witness of our conscience (Romans 2:14–16). Though God speaks through his creation and our consciences, they're insufficient on their own. Our sinful nature distorts their witness, and they lack the specifics needed to know the person and work of Christ in the gospel. This is one reason why these types of revelation are called "general." They're general in the sense that they reveal God to all people in all places, but they're also general in what they reveal about God. To know God sufficiently, we need specific or "special revelation." This comes through Christ and his Word.

Hebrews 1:1–2 makes it clear that Jesus is the greatest revelation of God. He is the "image of the invisible God" (Colossians 1:15), and he is the Word made flesh (John 1:14). He speaks the words of the Father and does what he sees his Father doing (John 5:19). This is why Jesus says, "Whoever has seen me has seen the Father" (John 14:9). Though Jesus is the greatest revealer of God, he is no longer physically present on earth. If we can't see Jesus, how can we know him or the Father? Through his Word.

Throughout history, God spoke directly to his people. He spoke to Adam, Noah, Abraham, Moses, etc. His words revealed specific things about his nature and will. As he spoke, certain men were carried along by the Holy Spirit and wrote down his Word (2 Peter 1:20–21). The Spirit's supernatural work in the writing of Scripture makes it special. It's the very Word of God breathed out by him and written through human authors (2 Timothy 3:16). In Scripture, we come to know the Son, who reveals the Father through the work of the Spirit. Because the Bible is God's Word, it will never fail, never fade, and never fall short in accomplishing its purpose (Isaiah 40:8; 55:10–11). God's Word should be the primary source we use to teach kids theology because it is the means through which God has promised to teach us about himself.

Guardrails or train tracks?

At this point, you might be thinking, *Of course we need to teach Scripture to know God! Who would deny this?* Sadly, the Bible is not as highly regarded as many might assume. Over the past several years, biblical illiteracy has been on the rise. According to research done by the American Bible Society, millions of Americans disengage from the Bible each year, meaning they don't use, listen to, read, or consider it when making decisions.[10] Millions! No doubt, this is having a negative impact on the church's ministry to children.

"But that's not my church!" you might protest. "We teach the Bible every week." That might be true, but even if your ministry engages the Bible weekly, the question you need to ask yourself is, "*How* are we engaging the Bible?" It's one thing to reference the Bible in a lesson; it's another thing entirely to use it as the primary source of all that is said and done. A curriculum for children might engage Scripture, but does it do so effectively?

There is no shortage of children's ministry curricula. Options abound! While this is a wonderful gift, it also calls for greater levels of discernment—not just in what curriculum is chosen but also in how it's used. Due to busy schedules and a lack of volunteers, many children's ministries rely heavily on their curriculum to do most of the work for them.

But is this wise? Should leaders and teachers completely set themselves on the tracks that their curriculum lays down?

I like to think of a curriculum as a pair of guardrails because the analogy perfectly balances the need for guidance and ownership. Curricula can provide a scope and sequence for teaching along with helpful activities, and like guardrails, they can keep leaders from wandering off course while giving them the freedom to stay in the driver's seat. However, many churches opt for a "plug and play" approach, which keeps leaders glued to the curriculum. They stick to it like a train to its tracks.

During our church's VBS one summer, I was tasked with teaching the Bible lessons. Due to the size of our building and number of kids registered for the event, I was on a rotation to teach the Bible to three different age groups: older elementary, younger elementary, and preschool. I spent many hours reviewing the lessons in the curriculum packet, ensuring I knew the material inside and out. After the first couple of nights of VBS, I realized the curriculum was not working well for the preschoolers and older elementary students. Some of the phrasing was too abstract for my preschoolers, and the suggested questions and activities weren't connecting well with the older elementary students, so I had to adjust. I didn't change the overall theme or big idea of the lessons in my adaptations. Those served as guardrails to keep my teaching clear and to keep my thoughts focused. I did change some phrasing, illustrations, and applications of the content to better meet the needs of the kids I was serving. If I had stuck to the curriculum like a train to its tracks, I would have driven that train straight toward disaster!

Teaching about God accurately requires us to see a curriculum as a guide subservient to Scripture, not vice versa. We must be willing to adapt, tweak, remove, and add to curricula as needed. This only happens if we study, put in the work, and keep God's Word at the forefront. We're not called to coast or follow curricula blindly. We're in the driver's seat and must ensure our kids are following Scripture where it leads. For this to happen, kid's ministry leaders need to put in their own study apart from and alongside the curriculum they are given. This might seem counterintuitive, since curricula are purchased to avoid extra work, but as I stated above, curricula are only helpful insofar as they speak clearly to the specific children you have in your classroom and, even more importantly, to the degree that they align with Scripture. You cannot know how well a resource aligns with Scripture unless you first study the passage being taught for yourself.

Context, content, and consequence

Maybe you're a new Christian or volunteer in children's ministry, and you're not sure how to study the Bible to the degree needed to evaluate a lesson within a kid's curriculum. Or you might be a veteran leader, but you've relied so heavily on curriculum that you're not confident in your ability to study a passage apart from its use. Wherever you land on the spectrum, I want to provide you with a simple method to help you study a biblical passage or story so that you can consult Scripture thoughtfully and compare it to the teaching found within your curriculum.

Context can be defined as "the situation within which something exists or happens that can help explain it."[11] Since the Bible was written thousands of years ago across various cultures and peoples, considering the cultural context in which a biblical passage was written is necessary to understand its meaning. Ask contextual questions such as the following: "Who? What? When? Where? and Why?" You might ask, "Who wrote this passage, and to whom was it written? When was it written? Where does this passage take place? What took place before this passage? Why was this passage written?"

Part of the answers to these cultural and historical questions can come from reading a verse in its literary context. This means reading a verse, story, or passage in the context of the book in which it was written. Aside from reading the entire chapter or book you are studying, there are other resources you can reference to help you understand the context of a passage. Blueletterbible.org offers a variety of free tools, such as dictionaries, commentaries, and word studies, to help you understand the verse you are studying. The Bible Project produces summary videos that provide helpful overviews of every book of the Bible.[12] Using these tools can aid you in situating the passage you are teaching.

Once you have a grasp of the context, you can consider the content of your text. Content refers to the truth your passage intends to teach about God and all things in relation to him. When unearthing the content of your passage, you need to answer the "God question": What is happening in this passage, and what does it reveal about God? What does it reveal about his nature, character, and works in our world, and what does that reveal about us?

We are not only to be hearers of the word but doers as well (James 1:22). This means that every interaction we have with God's Word should have consequences for our lives. Once we have seen what a passage reveals about God's character and ways, we can ask the "So what?" question. How should the content change our lives? Are there prayers that we need to pray? Sins that we need to confess? Promises we need to keep? Actions we need to take? Words we need to speak? Thoughts we need to change? Whenever we encounter God's truth, we need to apply that truth as honestly and specifically as possible.

Technically, this Bible study method has four parts: "Context, Content, Christ, and Consequence," but we will deal with the Christ portion of this method in chapter 4. For now, the steps outlined above can help you begin studying Scripture for yourself so you can evaluate your curriculum and teach the Bible faithfully. You can also check out *A Short Guide to Reading the Bible Better* by George H. Guthrie to learn more about biblical study.[13]

Teaches of God—the right object

Good theology is not only taught by God but also teaches of God. Again, this might sound obvious, but as we saw in chapter 1, society has a very warped understanding of who God is. Good theology seeks to teach God as he has revealed himself, not as we would like him to be.

When it comes to kids, we can easily fall into the trap of teaching principles and morals without diving into doctrines of the faith. We can teach kids to be nice, kind, and generous, but if we aren't teaching them about God's character, will, and ways, we're feeding them an imbalanced meal. Good theology teaches the whole counsel of God's Word and puts the emphasis on the right things. To do this faithfully, we need to see what a Bible lesson teaches about God and then have every supporting element of our ministry highlight or reinforce it.

The flower technique

Most curricula provide games, crafts, and activities that accompany their lessons, but many of these supporting elements often highlight an aspect of a biblical story and not the meaning or point of the story. For example, I was teaching a lesson on Nehemiah, and the curriculum had a craft about the wall, an activity about teamwork, and an application point on leadership. Are these things wrong? No, but they're disjointed. If I were to have used these elements, the kids might have remembered aspects of Nehemiah's story, but they would have struggled to see how they all relate to God.

The primary goal of teaching the story of Nehemiah is not to tell kids to be like Nehemiah. The goal of the story is to teach them something about God through the life of Nehemiah. A teacher's job is to determine what that "something" is and have the supporting elements restate it repeatedly.

Some know this form of communication, which drives home a single point, as the "flower technique."[14] Imagine a simple flower in which the center circle represents your main idea and the connecting petals represent your accompanying illustrations, crafts, activities, etc. For the flower to be complete, each petal would need to connect to the center circle. Likewise, when teaching a Bible passage, you would want to ensure that every element (or petal) of your lesson flows out of and comes back to the main idea of the passage being taught (the center circle).

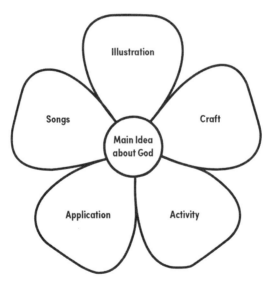

Figure 3. The Flower Technique

As you prepare to teach a lesson to your kids, you need to ask yourself, "What is the bottom line? What is the one idea

I'm trying to get across? What is the one thing I want my kids to remember from this lesson?" The big idea or bottom line should always be about God in some way. If your kids can remember your illustrations or the details of a story but are unable to remember what they communicate about God, then the bottom line is either off, unclear, or not stated enough.

The main point of our lessons should always be Christ-centered, or our lessons will inevitably become man-centered. Bottom lines that are man-centered say things like, "Be kind to your neighbor," "love others," or "you can be brave." Not only do these statements put the focus on us and what we can do, but they also don't require a commitment to Scripture or reliance on God. A PBS cartoon could just as easily make the above statements as the main point of an episode. Christ-centeredness orbits around the God of Scripture and pulls kids toward a life of ever-growing reliance on his strength and wisdom.

This isn't to say we can't make practical applications or highlight the godly characteristics exemplified in the Bible. As we'll see in chapter 3, theology is inherently practical. What we're stressing here is the need to have the correct main idea and focus of a biblical passage. If the main idea is wrong, then the application will be skewed. Every action, character, and moment must be seen, evaluated, and applied in light of who God reveals himself to be.

After all, we can't expect our kids' view of God to grow each week in our churches if we aren't explicitly pointing to God every time we teach them. We should make it hard for kids to say, "I don't know," when asked what they learned at church. We should be communicating a specific truth about God clearly and memorably each week. If we're not, then we're not teaching good theology. He's the object of our worship, devotion, and teaching. Everything should be designed to point to, highlight, and explain who he is.

Leads to glorifying God—the right goal

Good theology has the right source, object, and goal, which is God's glory. Pleasing him should be the "why" behind everything we do. If his honor isn't our primary motive, filter, and destination, then our ministries will ask bad questions, make poor decisions, and pursue lackluster goals.

When teaching the Bible, having God's glory as our goal leads us to ask, "How do I teach this faithfully?" before asking, "How do I teach this creatively?" God's glory also cultivates the humility needed to say, "I don't know," when a child asks a question we can't answer, and it pushes us to pursue what is true over what is easy.

Building coat racks for the glory of God

One way we pursue truth over ease is through the language we use to describe God. As we saw in chapter 1, God's greatness is minimized through cheap explanations. A common example of minimization can be seen in how children's books and curricula present the doctrine of the Trinity. Many try to explain the Trinity through various analogies like eggs, plants, or water. While these illustrations seem harmless on the surface, we need to ask ourselves, "Are they accurate?" It might seem helpful to compare our triune God to the three parts of an egg or the three states of water, but these analogies state things about God that are not only untrue but misrepresent God to a dangerous degree. It's better to give faithful language that is harder to explain than to give easy examples that distort who God is.

If theology is literally "God-talk," our job is to give kids the most accurate language possible when we are discussing God. Providing our kids with theological language is like placing a coat rack in a Southern home. Since winters are short and mild in the South, heavy coats are rarely worn, making coat racks appear useless. However, when those rare snow days come, having a hook on which to hang your coat is beneficial. The same is true with language and ideas about God.

When we expose our children to certain doctrines, they may not understand them immediately, and that's OK! We need to recognize that some truths are taught purely for the sake of exposure. In doing this, we provide children with mental hooks on which their theological thoughts can hang.

The doctrine of the Trinity serves as a great example of this. The tri-unity of our God is beautiful, but it's highly abstract, especially for younger children. Most illustrations of the Trinity either undervalue his oneness (the illustration of an egg) or convolute his persons (the illustration of a man with multiple roles). Even the analogies that seek to be faithful lean more toward upholding the mystery of the Trinity than easily explaining it.[15] Since God is holy and therefore fundamentally different from us, we should expect to encounter truths about him that are hard to contain in nice, neat packages. Sometimes, the best thing we can do is plainly speak the truth and pray that our children's understanding will catch up with the concepts we've passed on to them. Again, this doesn't mean we avoid the hard work of finding words, phrases, or examples to explain concepts as clearly as possible, but we must never diminish God's mystery at the expense of accessibility.

Because God's glory is on the line, we want what we say about him to be correct before it is clever. One of the best ways to do this is through a story. The doctrine of the Trinity states there is one God in three persons. That's a simple explanation of the Trinity, but it's still abstract. However, in the context of the gospel story, the abstract becomes more concrete. The gospel tells us there is only one God who can save us, and the doctrine of the Trinity reveals that this one

God saves us in three persons. God the Father sent God the Son to die and rise in place of sinners, and God the Spirit is sent by the Father and the Son to live in believers and make them new. It's not a story about three gods who save us, nor is it a story about one person who saves us. The gospel is the story of salvation given to us by one God in three persons.[16]

Though the short gospel story above makes the doctrine of the Trinity more concrete, it can still be hard for preschoolers and younger elementary children to understand. That's why we want to do our best to provide faithful language. When the time comes for their understanding to catch up with their language, we want to ensure that we've provided them with strong theological hooks on which the coats of their understanding can rest.

Illustrations and mental leaps

Seeking accuracy doesn't mean that our teaching has to be bland or monotonous. We don't glorify God when we speak of him in a dull, unthinking manner. Illustrations and object lessons can be great tools for teaching theology in engaging, memorable ways, but these tools can work against us if we don't use them wisely. The goal of an illustration isn't to purely dazzle kids and get their attention but to illuminate and clarify the truth. That said, we should avoid making our stories or object lessons overly elaborate.

Once, when teaching preschoolers, the curriculum I was using suggested playing a video at the start of the lesson. The video began with a girl telling a story that was designed to connect with the main idea of the lesson. However, after her story, she began giving details of the Bible story in the lessons, including the hard-to-pronounce names of people and places. After she was done listing the names and locations, she referred to her story and how it tied to the truth the kids were going to learn. Needless to say, my preschoolers were lost. They got so hung up on the list of funny-sounding names of people and places, that they forgot parts of the girl's story and the main idea of the lesson entirely. The reason this video failed to deliver is that it was too complicated. It had too many elements and was overly elaborate in certain aspects. Because of this, the kids in my group couldn't connect the dots between the illustration of her story and the main idea of the lesson.

When using objects or illustrations, we should try to get from point A to point B as smoothly as possible. There needs to be a direct correlation between the illustration and the concept, not a multi-step or indirect correlation between them. Being both precise and concise in our illustrations will not only serve our kids in making truth clear, but it will also aid in making truth memorable.

Experiences and the power of emotions

God created humans with emotions, and we glorify him in our teaching when we engage kids' emotions, instead of ignoring them. In fact, emotions have a powerful tie to a child's ability to learn and recall information. The human brain has limited storage and uses mechanisms to determine what is worth holding on to and remembering. If feelings of great joy or fear are associated with an event or piece of information, the emotions serve as a signal to our brains that the event or info is worth remembering. This is why teachers should employ methods that engage children emotionally in the truths they are teaching. Nothing does this like experiences. What do we mean by experiences? Anything that allows children to experience in some way the concept being taught.

For example, I once taught the doctrine of sin to a group of elementary-age kids and wanted them to experience how they fall short of God's glory. Toward the end of my lesson,

I gave the children each a piece of paper and challenged them to fold their papers in half ten times. Whoever could beat the challenge would be deemed the winner. The children laughed, thinking the challenge would be easy, but after a few folds, they found it to be much more difficult than they had anticipated. I even had other leaders come to the front and try it, and they failed as well. After each kid attempted the challenge, I had them give their papers to the other leaders, and said, "None of us could beat the challenge, could we? We all fell short of the goal. In the same way, we all fall short of God's glory. We all sin and fail to meet God's goodness and perfection. Because of this, we deserve punishment and are unable to live with God forever in heaven." I concluded the lesson by pointing to Christ, who didn't fall short of God's glory but displayed it perfectly. He is sinless, yet he died for sinners so that those who fall short of God's glory and goodness can be saved in order to experience that glory and goodness to the fullest.

To this day, if I bump into kids who were in the class during this lesson, they bring up the paper challenge and how Jesus saves us from sin. I think they remember it because the emotion of frustration they felt when they were unable to complete the seemingly easy challenge caused their brains to hold onto the experience AND the truth taught in conjunction with it. Teaching through experiences can aid teachers in distilling doctrine because that method of teaching pushes them to connect their concepts to concrete activities, and the more concrete we can make theology, the more likely our kids will be able to understand and retain it.

Mature in Christ

We've learned that theology is the application of God's revelation to all of life. This means that everyone is a theologian—either a good one or a bad one. As theologians, we will be held accountable for the type of theology we teach our kids. Will you be found faithful? Can you, along with Paul, say, "Him we proclaim, warning everyone and teaching everyone with all wisdom, that we may present everyone mature in Christ" (Colossians 1:28). Is that your desire? To present every child under your care mature in Christ? Are you in anguish until Christ is formed in them (Galatians 4:19)?

Any other goal or cry of the heart is not only misguided—it's dangerous. It's a weak foundation built on sand. Unless God is rightly taught and highly honored, our ministries are nothing more than glorified babysitting services. Of course, we want to have fun. Of course, we want to create memorable experiences and connect with kids on their level. But if we get so consumed with the activities of ministry that they eclipse the glory of Christ, we implicitly teach our kids that Jesus is a stepping stone, not the cornerstone, of their lives. Leaders and parents, speak the truth in love to your children so that they grow up in Christ in every way (Ephesians 4:15). He is the source, object, and goal of all things. As missionary C. T. Studd beautifully said, "Only one life, 'twill soon be past. Only what's done for Christ shall last."[17] May this anthem echo in your hearts as you prepare lessons and proclaim God's gospel and Word to your children.

Discussion Questions

1. Everyone is a theologian. How should this truth change the way parents, Sunday school teachers, and ministry leaders perceive their roles and teach kids?

2. Theology is described as an ecosystem of faith in which various doctrines (or teachings) depend on one another. How can this understanding of theology help you better study God's Word and teach your kids?

3. Several analogies were used for teaching good theology to kids, such as guardrails, the flower technique, building

coatracks, and mental leaps. Which one of these stood out to you the most and why?

4. Our goal as theologians is to present everyone mature in Christ (Colossians 1:28). How can you keep this at the forefront of your ministry?

Chapter 3

Theological Fluency: Applying Theology to All of Life

I (Hunter) was a decent student in high school. I generally paid attention, got good grades, and saw value in what I was learning—except for algebra. That was a different story. In algebra, I struggled to focus, earned terrible grades, and dreaded going to class. It was bad—so bad that I had to start meeting with my teacher after school to get tutored.

In our first tutoring session, the teacher looked at me, perplexed, and asked, "Hunter, why do you think you're doing so poorly in my class? You excel in your other classes but barely get by in this one. Why do you think that is?" On the outside, I sheepishly replied, "I don't know," but on the inside, I was shouting, "Because it's pointless!"

With time, I eventually voiced my frustration with the class. "It doesn't seem practical," I said. "If I'm not going to use any of this stuff in the real world, why do I need to learn it?" My teacher responded with reasons that she deemed satisfactory, but I remained unconvinced. Despite my skepticism, I muscled through the tutoring sessions and completed the class with a decent grade. I never saw the value of that class and perceived it to be nothing more than a random subject I learned to please my teacher and progress through school.

Believers can perceive theology in a similar way. They know it's essential for understanding God and serving the church, but its implications for the everyday moments of life can seem vague—even irrelevant. With the challenges kids face, such as anxiety, bullying, and sexual identity, doctrines like the Trinity and Christ's ascension can seem . . . well . . . impractical. Why study and spend time teaching these doctrines if they don't appear to speak to our kids' immediate needs? This isn't a bad question. It's just built on a faulty assumption—namely, that most doctrines are too lofty or theoretical to be immediately applicable to the modern challenges our children experience. I think this flawed assumption is a by-product of how we approach theology and Christianity as a whole.

THE PROBLEM: COMPARTMENTALIZED BELIEFS

Though I disliked algebra for its apparent lack of usefulness, another class was just as impractical, though I saw it as applicable at the time. That class was Spanish. I remember thinking it would be useful since Spanish is the second most dominant language in the United States. Though I wasn't the best student, I studied hard and came out of the class with an A.

Despite my good grades, I couldn't speak a lick of Spanish. I could recite the Spanish alphabet by memory, conjugate verbs, and translate phrases on paper, but if someone tried to converse with me, I would look at them like a deer in the headlights. Why? Because I was familiar with aspects of the language but not fluent in it. I could repeat phrases, but I couldn't carry on a conversation. I wasn't fluent because I didn't consistently speak the language outside of class hours. Since I relegated its use to specific times and places, I didn't think in Spanish, dream in Spanish, or intuitively hear or speak the language. I would think or talk in English first, then awkwardly try to rethink and speak the concept in Spanish. It was highly unnatural. Compartmentalizing the use and study of Spanish to one part of my life unintentionally made it impractical in others.

The same can happen in our approach to theology. We know it's important, and we might even say it's practical, but treating it like one subject of study among many compartmentalizes it. And once something is compartmentalized (like my Spanish class), it inevitably becomes impractical. This is why we spent so much time in chapter 2 unpacking what theology is. If theology is only defined as the "study of God," then it can be approached as a subject that is only studied at certain times and spaces, such as church services or Bible studies. But theology isn't merely a subject we look at—it's truth we look through. It's a lens through which we should view ourselves and the world.[1] Put another way, theology doesn't just teach us how to think about God; it helps us think God's thoughts after him. It helps us to see all spheres of life through his eyes and understand them according to his truth.

The psalmist had this in mind when he said, "For with you is the fountain of life; in your light do we see light" (Psalm 36:9). Only when we see things by God's light do we see them as they truly are. C. S. Lewis echoed these thoughts when he said, "I believe in Christianity as I believe that the Sun has risen, not only because I see it, but because by it I see everything else."[2]

Jesus is not one subject among many but the light and lens by which all subjects are rightly seen and understood. When we present Christ in this way to our children, we help them become theologically fluent. Their "God-Talk" won't become a second language relegated to certain contexts or settings but the primary language they use to think and speak within every moment, space, and interaction.

Worldviews and video games

How we think, speak, and act flows out of our view of the world (or worldview for short). It might seem odd to mention worldview in a book about teaching theology to kids, but the reality is that everyone has a worldview, including kids. Truthfully, the elementary years are the primary time when a person's worldview is being formed. Researcher George Barna says, "Between 15 to 18 months of age is when most children start forming their worldview. By the age of 13, it's almost completely in place."[3] Let that sink in. If a person's view of the world is primarily set by age thirteen, most people are living out of the worldview constructed during their elementary years (the age range of the kids in your Sunday school classes and children's ministries). This means that the volunteers serving in our children's ministries are not only theologians and disciple makers—they are worldview shapers! If this is the role and calling of Bible teachers and parents, then we must understand what a worldview is.

Many books have been written on worldview, and even more definitions exist. Despite the ever-growing number of articles, blogs, and books on the subject, most agree on the general idea that a worldview is a set of assumptions that determine how one perceives and lives in the world. These assumptions or beliefs dictate how we make judgments and behave in situations. Thus, if a person has a Christian worldview, his values, behavior, and decisions will be made in light of biblical truth and presuppositions.

Though I'm not much of a video game player, I enjoy all things *Super Mario*. The games are fun, creative, and keep things interesting through the use of "worlds." If you've ever played a *Super Mario* game, you know that Mario has to go through different worlds to save Princess Peach. Each world has its own structure, themes, and rules of gameplay, although certain fundamental rules remain consistent throughout the game. In one portion of the game, you inhabit an ice world with slippery floors that make running and jumping a goofy (and frustrating) experience. In another part of the game, you occupy a water world that completely replaces the running and jumping functions for swimming and diving. Each world changes how Mario operates and relates to his surroundings.

In a similar way, the worldviews we adopt and uphold dictate how we operate in our world. A person thinks, lives, and evaluates reality differently in a Christian worldview than he would in an Islamic, Buddhist, or atheistic worldview. Of course, the analogy breaks down slightly since Christians don't live in a different world than those of other belief systems, but while Christians may not live in a different world, they see the world differently. This makes a difference . . . a world of difference (pun intended).

You get the point. Everyone has a worldview, and worldviews impact every detail and decision of our lives. Since people's views of God completely alter their worldviews, this makes theology incredibly practical. Our doctrines influence our decisions. Our beliefs drive our behaviors, and our affections motivate our actions. No matter how theoretical or lofty it may appear, all theology is practical for us and our kids. Dr. John Tweeddale summarizes this nicely:

> The study of theology is important because what you believe about God affects everything in your life: your studies, your vocation, your worldview, your eating habits, your hobbies, your marriage, your friendships, and much, much more. There is not an area of life that is not impacted by your theology.[4]

A buffet of beliefs

Sadly, many children's ministry pastors don't have a consistent biblical worldview. The Cultural Research Center made the shocking discovery that 12 percent of children's pastors have a biblical worldview.[5] Only 12 percent! Respondents were asked fifty-four worldview-related questions, which fell into eight different categories of belief and behavior. Of those eight categories, children's pastors scored the lowest in the category of the "Bible, Truth, and Morals." They also scored low in the categories of "Human Character and Nature" and "Lifestyle, Behavior, Relationships." What do you notice from these findings? Do you see the correlation between a low view of Scripture and a lackluster understanding of morals and behavior? A consistently Christian worldview matters greatly.

I say "consistently Christian worldview" because the respondents weren't full-blown atheists. They claimed to believe in Christ and scored well in certain points of Christian belief. But how can a person answer like a Christian in one category and a nonbeliever in another? The answer is syncretism. This is the process of combining opposing ideas, religious beliefs, or practices.

I liken it to a buffet of beliefs. In a buffet-style restaurant, customers are given a variety of food options from which to choose. A person could have fried chicken, Thai dumplings, deviled eggs, spaghetti, and soft-serve ice cream on a single plate. It's a smorgasbord of opposing flavors held together by a person's culinary preferences.

When it comes to beliefs, people often do the same thing. They're exposed to various ideas and choose the ones that fit their mental and emotional taste buds. This isn't always done intentionally and often comes as the result of compartmentalized living. When life is seen in segments and not as a whole, opposing beliefs can be held together unknowingly. If the Christian faith is seen as an accessory and not as an all-encompassing worldview, it leads to a faith that is both impractical and inconsistent, and an inconsistent faith is a dangerous faith.

The fruit reveals the root

The statistics above might have you in a panic. You might be wondering, *Do I have a consistent Christian worldview? Am I part of the 12 percent?* Before you get lost in your thoughts, I want to encourage you with the truth that Jesus has provided us with a way to examine the desires and beliefs of our hearts. It's found in Luke 6:43–45:

> "For no good tree bears bad fruit, nor again does a bad tree bear good fruit, for each tree is known by its own fruit. For figs are not gathered from thorn-bushes, nor are grapes picked from a bramble bush. The good person out of the good treasure of his heart produces good, and the evil person out of his evil treasure produces evil, for out of the abundance of the heart his mouth speaks."

Jesus's metaphor is brilliant and provides a timeless principle for exposing the condition of our hearts. The fruit of our lives reveals the root of our hearts. More bluntly, our actions reveal our true beliefs. There's a difference between what we claim to believe and what we actually believe. We can claim to believe one thing yet expose our true beliefs through the content of our lives.

Paul David Tripp elaborates on this truth in his book *Do You Believe?*:

> Many of us are willing to live with functional inconsistency between the truths that we declare we believe and how we choose to live. So it must be said that the truths you actually believe are the truths that you live because faith is never just intellectual assent. . . . Truth not lived is truth not believed.[6]

If you want to pass down a consistently Christian faith to the kids in your ministry, it begins with an examination of your own heart. Where have you planted the roots of your belief? Here are some questions to help you unearth your roots.

- What am I living for? What am I striving after?
- What do I run to for answers? Who or what do I look to for help?
- Where do I turn for comfort?
- What motivates my decisions?
- How do I define success?
- Who or what has the greatest amount of influence in my life?
- How do I spend my free time?
- What brings me joy? What frustrates me? What leads to sorrow?
- What consumes my thoughts? What do I naturally talk about?
- How do I spend my money? What dictates my saving and spending?

Take a few moments, put down this book, and pause. Think of how you answered these questions. As the roots of your heart are exposed, ask God to help you uproot inconsistent beliefs and plant roots in the good soil of his truth. Allow God to speak to you, orient your focus, and rehabilitate your loves.

THE PRINCIPLE: THEOLOGY IS PRACTICAL

Now that we've diagnosed the problem, we're in a better place to consider the principle. Practical theology flows out of a consistent theology—a congruent system of belief that colors everything we see, from the monumental to the mundane.

To see the practical implications of a doctrine, we need to see what a particular passage or truth teaches about God and everything in relation to him. Let's look at a few doctrines and ask these simple questions:

- How does this truth about God change the way I think about *myself*?
- How does this truth about God change the way I think about *others*?
- How does this truth about God change the way I think about the *world*?

The goal is to take a doctrine and apply it to a specific sphere of life. As you study, you could formulate the practical application by filling in the blanks below.

- How does the truth about _____ (insert doctrine) change the way I think about _____ (insert sphere of life)?

Doctrine: God created all things

The Bible begins with a declaration that God created all things (Genesis 1:1). Since God created all things, he owns all things (Psalm 24:1–2; Job 41:11). As Creator and Owner, he also establishes the value and standard of all things (see, for example, Genesis 1:31). With these truths in mind, we can use our questions above to parse out practical applications.

How does the truth about **God as the Creator** change the way I think about **myself**?

- Since God is the Creator, and I am not, he determines my identity. Contrary to the ideas of modern culture, identity isn't something we make. It's given (Galatians 2:20; 2 Corinthians 5:17; 1 Peter 2:9). I'm not the creator of my own meaning and destiny. God

gives everything I do meaning, and his glory is the purpose of all my endeavors.
- This is an important message for our children to understand since most of today's movies, TV shows, and advertisements promote the opposite. Kids are told to follow their hearts and make their dreams come true instead of following God's desire for their lives and having their dreams and aspirations align with his purpose for them.

How does the truth about **God as the Creator** change the way I think about **others**?
- Because God made people in his image, they have intrinsic value and worth. This means that a person's value isn't determined by age or ability but by the fact that they are made in God's image (Genesis 1:26–27).
- This truth speaks directly to bullying and human equality. We are called to love others because they are made in God's image. We can pray for our enemies and treat those who are different from us with respect and dignity.
- No other belief system or religion provides a better framework for human dignity and worth than Christianity. The doctrine of the image of God is invaluable and dramatically influences how we relate to others.

How does the truth about **God as the Creator** change the way I think about the **world**?
- Since God owns all things, and everything I own is a gift from him, I should live generously and open-handedly with all I have (2 Corinthians 9:6–11; James 1:17).

- Today's "hustle" culture flies in the face of this truth. Those who deny God's existence believe this world is all they have. Therefore, they think they have to work furiously to get everything they can in this life. This leads to a greedy, self-focused mindset.
- As Christians, we work hard, but we don't do so to hoard treasure or build our own little kingdoms. We do so to honor God with our time and abilities (Colossians 3:17). This world is God's world, and as his image bearers, we should seek to be good stewards of the people, places, and things he's entrusted to us.

You might be thinking, *That's an easy doctrine to apply to our kids' lives. What about a more abstract doctrine like the self-sufficiency of God?* I'm glad you asked! Let's see how this doctrine changes the way we look at ourselves, others, and the world!

Doctrine: The aseity (self-sufficiency) of God

As we saw above, God is the Creator of all things. This means that nothing created God. He isn't dependent on anything or anyone. Simply put, God doesn't need us (Acts 17:24–25). He is sufficient within himself. This doctrine closely relates to the fact that God is eternal. He doesn't have a beginning, and he doesn't have an ending (Psalm 90:2). He always has been, and he always will be!

How does the truth about **God's aseity** change the way I think about **myself**?

- Since God is self-sufficient, he doesn't need our worship or love to fill a need within himself or to make him whole. This is good news! Why? Since God is self-sufficient, his love isn't dependent on what we offer him. His faithfulness isn't fickle, nor is his love sporadic.

- This truth can provide peace to anxious hearts in an unpredictable world. Seasons change. People fail. But the self-sufficient God is constant. He does not depend on anyone for comfort and life, but he is the ultimate source of comfort and life to those who rest in him.

How does the truth about God's aseity change the way I think about others?

- God doesn't need humans to flourish, but we do! As dependent creatures, we need others not only to survive physically but to thrive spiritually. It wasn't good for Adam to be alone in the bliss of the garden, and it isn't good for us to be alone in our fallen world. God has designed us to thrive in community.
- This is why participating in a local church is so important! As the members of the church use their spiritual gifts to serve one another, the body of Christ grows and matures (1 Corinthians 12:12–31).

How does the truth about God's aseity change the way I think about the world?

- Being self-sufficient, God is eternal. The things of this world will wither and fade, but God and his Word will last forever (Isaiah 40:6–8). Since God is the only one who will never change or decay, we should place our hopes, dreams, and successes on him.
- Having a growing career is wonderful, but it doesn't last. Being an all-star baseball player is exciting, but it's not eternal. Kids try to find success in their good grades or worth in others' opinions. But the

only truth that can provide comfort in life and
death is that they belong, both body and soul, to the
all-powerful, self-sufficient Savior (1 Corinthians
6:19–20; see also the first question and answer of the
Heidelberg Catechism).

We could spend multiple chapters mining the implications of these truths, but hopefully these few examples have
given you a glimpse of the innumerable ways theology applies
to the lives of you and your children.

We encourage you to practice this for yourself. Pick
a truth about God and a sphere of life, and see how many
points of application you can make. You can even get more
specific with the sphere of life and apply truth to the areas of
work, school, marriage, etc. The more you practice, the more
natural (or fluent) you will become in seeing and understanding things theologically.

THE PRACTICE: DEVELOP THEOLOGICAL DISCERNMENT

In chapter 2, we emphasized the truth that everyone is a theologian. We all have a knowledge of God, and that knowledge, whether true or distorted, affects how we think and
live. This means that a good theologian seeks to know God
correctly and live rightly in light of his truth.

Alister McGrath defines the role of a theologian as
"someone who cultivates the habit of discernment: seeing
things rightly, properly and fully."[7] I love this! I think it's an
especially pertinent definition for our children. After all, isn't
this what we want for them? To be discerning in a world
full of fake news and false gospels? To distinguish truth from
error, right from wrong, and, as Charles Spurgeon is credited
as saying, "the difference between right and *almost* right?"[8]

We want our kids to do more than just acquire knowledge, we want them to apply the right knowledge in the right
way at the right time. But our world works against this goal.

Our culture conditions our kids toward distraction, not discernment. If we want to develop theological discernment in our children, we must intentionally fight for it in our church services, classrooms, small groups, and homes. Here are some tips to help you teach theology with an eye toward wisdom and practical application.

Pose open-ended questions

Questions are one of a teacher's best tools. They not only help leaders gauge a group's understanding but they also serve as a bridge between knowledge and application. While questions are powerful, they can easily be misused. Closed questions, answered with a simple "yes" or "no," aren't always bad, but they're rarely best. Sprinkling open-ended questions throughout your teaching time can increase engagement and develop wisdom.

One night, as I was putting my kids to bed, I was having difficulty getting them to calm down before our bedtime prayer (can anyone relate?). In the flurry of many shushes, I said, "I'm trying to talk to God, and I want us to be respectful as I speak to him." For some reason, the words I said made me pause. I had an overwhelming sense of God's realness, for lack of a better word. Before I began praying, I looked at each of my kids and asked, "Do you think God is real or pretend?" Immediately, my oldest daughter, Margot (who was five years old at the time), shouted, "He's real!" I turned to her and asked, "How do you know he's real?" She looked up at the ceiling, thought for a moment, and then said, "Well, without God, there's nothing." She thought again, then continued, "God made everything, so if he's pretend, then we wouldn't have anything." Her response blew me away. I didn't teach her to say this, nor had I prepared her for it. We taught her the creation story and lived as if God were real, but posing the open-ended question gave her the opportunity to connect the dots between what she knew about God and what she experienced in the world.

Wisdom is all about connection—connecting what you know to what you experience. When we pose open-ended questions, it helps our kids develop the skill of making theological connections in their everyday lives. God is not a summary of ideas. He's a person, and our job as teachers and parents is to help our kids encounter the person of God wherever they are and in whatever they're doing.

Paint pictures

Open-ended questions are good, but they're only one tool in your bag of teaching elements. Another complementary tool at your disposal is a paintbrush—not a literal paintbrush but an imaginary one. Let me explain.

Questions are sometimes met with blank stares or awkward silence. Sometimes, this happens due to the difficulty of the question. The question we are asking might be too advanced for the children we're teaching, or we might not have provided enough content for the question to make sense. Questions can also be met with uncertainty because of their vagueness.

For example, let's say you've just taught a lesson on Christ's sacrificial love, and you want to help them apply this truth to their lives. If you ask them, "How can you show sacrificial love this week?" the responses will most likely be shaky or off-topic. You might get a few general answers, but most kids will probably respond with unsure looks. Why? Because the question is too broad. A week is a vague concept, and kids are concrete thinkers. They need specific moments and scenarios in which they can place themselves. Obscure questions are like abstract art, while our kids need finely painted pictures that help them see the application of truth in vibrant ways.

So let's paint pictures. Instead of asking your kids, "How can you show sacrificial love this week?" ask them, "How can you show sacrificial love to your parents when you get home from school?" Get even more specific. Ask the kids who play sports how they can show sacrificial love to their teammates on the soccer or baseball field. Ask siblings how they can show their brothers and sisters sacrificial love during play, dinner, or bedtime. A powerful question will be specific in its formulation yet open in its responses. Painting these types of questions frees up your children to respond with confidence and curiosity.

Push practices

Theology is practical, but it's not always intuitive. Sometimes, kids need a push in the right direction to understand the implications of a biblical text. Another way to say this is that kids need a filter through which they can process the truths they're learning. Spiritual disciplines or practices serve as both a nudge and a filter for our kids. Practices such as prayer, Bible reading, singing, and the like are trusted tools we should utilize every chance we get. They provide immediate applications to a lesson and give our kids ways to engage the truths they've been handed.

Returning to our previous example on sacrificial love, let's consider practices through which we can push the truths of this lesson. You might utilize the practice of prayer by having your kids thank God for the sacrificial love he has shown in Christ or by asking God to help them demonstrate Christ's sacrificial love to the people in their lives. You could also practice Scripture memory and play a game that aids your kids in memorizing a passage about God's love or how believers are to show love through him. You could also practice service by giving your kids time during the lesson to write notes of encouragement to the elderly members of your church. The options are endless. Thinking through how a lesson's principles or truths can be applied through various spiritual practices gives your kids a filter to push beyond knowledge into engagement.

Present objections

This last tip is geared more toward older elementary and is a tool that should be utilized more frequently with middle and high school students. As kids get older, they realize their peers don't always think or make choices like they do. They learn that other kids are raised to believe in different gods or that some haven't grown up believing in a god at all. It can be helpful to periodically present objections that your older kids can ponder.

You can use this tool by starting with the phrase, "Some say . . ." Then present an objection a person or group might have against the truth you've taught. For example, I was teaching about the birth of Christ to a group of kids and explained that Jesus is God who became a man. As I neared the end of the lesson, I said, "Some say that Jesus wasn't really God. Some people believe that he was a good person but wasn't God become man." I wrapped things up by restating the big idea of the lesson and reminding them that Jesus could only save sinners if he is both God and man. That's it. That may not seem like a big deal, but peppering in little comments like this can prepare our kids for objections they might encounter by making them aware of those objections.

I use this tool sparingly and quickly because I don't want the objection to take away or distract from the truth being taught. I also don't want to spend too much time on objections because, as we saw earlier, the younger years are a highly formative time of worldview building in a person's life. I want to ensure my kids have a well-built understanding of the Christian worldview before spending a substantial amount of time comparing it with other worldviews and answering the objections of others.

Do kids need to be equipped to navigate the chaotic world around them? Absolutely! Do we want them to answer objections and be able to sniff out falsehood? You'd better believe it! But to do this well, kids need to know the Christian faith inside and out. We can't expect them to live out and defend a faith they don't know.

This is why theological fluency is essential to effective apologetics (defense of the faith). When kids are given a consistent biblical worldview through which they think, see, and interact with the world, they are better equipped to point out the lies and inconsistencies of opposing views.

The Christian faith is easier to uphold and defend when it is seen not only to be beautiful and true but also practical and good. May our kids experience the goodness of God as we teach them to see his beauty in all things and apply his truth to every fiber of their existence.

Discussion Questions

1. Theology isn't just a subject of study but a lens through which we look. How does understanding theology in this way change how you think about, study, and teach theology?

2. According to the Cultural Research Center at Arizona Christian University, only 12 percent of children's pastors have a consistently biblical worldview.[9] What do you think has led to this? What other worldviews do you believe are creeping into children's ministries unknowingly?

3. Theological fluency takes practice. To see the practical implications of theology, take the time to study the following doctrines and apply them to specific spheres of your life.

    a. Doctrines
- God is Omnipotent (All-Powerful)
- God is Omniscient (All-Knowing)
- God is Omnipresent (Present Everywhere at All Times)

    b. Application
- How does the truth about _____ (insert doctrine) change the way I think about _____ (insert sphere of life)?

4. Of the four tips given to aid you in developing theological discernment in your kids, which did you find most helpful and why?

    a. Pose Open-Ended Questions

    b. Paint Pictures

    c. Push Practices

    d. Present Objections

Chapter 4

Theology as Story

*Fairy tales are more than true: not because they tell us that
dragons exist, but because they tell us that dragons can be beaten.*
– G. K. Chesterton

There are two types of people in the world: people who read books and people who read shortened notes about books so they don't have to read books. I (Sam) am in the former group, and if you are this far into this book, I'm guessing you are as well. Stories are rich and complex. Notes about those stories are often true, factual, and cold. In high school I would read the stories, but many of my friends read the notes. We both passed the tests at the end, but without the context and the complexity, the story was only information to be regurgitated for a test for the notes-reading crowd. For me, stories were an invitation to wonder.

Most stories in Sunday school curricula that have been written for kids are stories taken from the Bible because they teach a truth that the teacher or pastor feels is needed for kids. A curriculum is often a collection of stories that well-meaning people have pulled from the Bible to help kids in their day-to-day lives and to get them familiar with the characters of the Bible.

This creates a sort of CliffsNotes Christianity—people who are familiar with the characters, the ideas, and some of the truths of the Bible but don't understand the message as a whole, the arc of Scripture in which all stories point toward Jesus, nor, most importantly, the God of the Bible.

The Bible isn't a tool for the betterment of our lives. It is the story of God for us. We are not central to the story of the Bible. Every good story, like the Bible, has a beginning, a middle, and an end. The Bible starts and ends with a God who is a powerful, preexisting Creator, Redeemer, and King.

THE PROBLEM: CLIFFSNOTES CHRISTIANITY

We live in a culture that loves CliffsNotes—quick, concise summaries of works of literature that help us grasp the main point and move on. We love tools like this because they save time, they help interpret lengthy passages that might be hard to understand, and they help us skirt potential boredom. But they cause us to miss the beauty of the mundane, the joy in the journey, and the details of the story. We feed our kids a diet of heroes and victories in the Bible but skip the laments and the hard stories because, somewhere along the way, we decided that those more difficult details were not for kids. The result is that we have generations of kids who have a CliffsNotes faith that can regurgitate a list of what Christians are supposed to say and believe but who are devoid of understanding the beauty that comes from the story—the story of God's redeeming love for them.

Why abridged Christianity is harmful

When we train our kids to look for facts and hunt for answers by reducing stories to the basic elements within them, we train them to miss the point. They might be able to tell you who was on Noah's boat, the number of animals that entered the boat, or who closed the door of the ark, but *stories* are much more profound. They locate those facts in time and space and give them substance.

One of the unexpected outcomes I have found through my journey through the humanities is that CliffsNotes kids at school may pass English class but they rarely become life-long readers of literature. This has implications for how we teach theology to kids.

Recently Lifeway Research conducted a survey of young adult Christians to try and find out which factors predict the highest spiritual condition. The top factor they highlighted was Bible reading. They explain, "Twenty-nine percent of the young adults regularly read the Bible while growing up, according to their parents. On average, that group has 12.5 percent higher spiritual health than otherwise comparable individuals who didn't."[1]

Abridged, CliffsNotes-style faith is based on information—good and true information, but consists of facts devoid of context, empty of the surrounding story. When you help kids situate those facts in the stories you tell, it helps you ask better questions like, "How does this passage of Scripture relentlessly point beyond me to Jesus?" and "How do I live in light of the truth this passage proclaims?"

When we take Bible stories and isolate them, we tend to look for nuggets of personally applicable truth rather than allowing the Bible to invite us into God's story—the true tale of God's love, our needs, God's supply, and ultimately, his glory.

We live in a world of excessive individualism. We can have most things we want in two days or less, thanks to the efficiency of online retailers and overnight shipping. Ads are focused on us; they are designed to appeal to our needs, wants, and desires. They relentlessly preach what we need to make our lives better.

If we are not wise and prayerful, we will do the same thing with God's story. The temptation is to save time, tell our kids the facts they need to know, and give them the

Reader's Digest version of every story. This approach can produce kids who know things about God but don't become lifelong students of his Word nor understand their place in his story.

> When we look at the Bible as information that can help us in life, we tend to displace the hero of the story (Christ) and put ourselves in the middle of the narrative. The results are tragic.

I remember thinking through a Bible story years ago, asking myself how it would help my kids be kinder or more honest. Both of those are good questions, but they are the wrong questions because they assume that we are the center of our own story and that the Bible is a tool to help us on our journey to find happiness around every corner. This is a profoundly unbiblical way of seeing. In placing ourselves at the center of each account in Scripture, we view God as coming alongside us to make our story better.

When we understand our story as finding its origin, meaning, and future hope in Christ's story, it profoundly changes how we live. It changes how we read the Bible and the stories we tell. The Bible does not primarily give us tools for our use but tells us a story of God's redeeming love for us in Christ.

Let me illustrate it this way. Kids love animals, so the stories of animals in the Bible are hot commodities. The most profoundly animal-centric story we love to tell kids is of the floating zoo—Noah's ark.

When we look at the story of Noah with ourselves in focus, we could end up saying things like this: "Noah loved God and worked hard every day building a boat. We need to be more like Noah and do our homework even when we feel like playing video games." This example may be an overexaggeration, but when we oversimplify the story and reduce it to facts and simplistic explanations without inviting kids to wonder or without giving them the bigger picture of how this narrative fits into the story of redemption, we have completely missed the point.

If, however, we tell the story of Noah not as facts and summaries but as one portion of a larger Story, we can show how it points beyond itself to the big picture of a merciful God breaking in to save men. The story of Noah is God's story. When we see it this way, everything changes. We see not only a God-loving, hard-working boatbuilder but we also see a faithful, long-suffering God who loves us not because we are good but because we are his.

We see God's love for Noah and his faithfulness as an extension of his covenant promise to Adam and Eve in Genesis 3. We see a completely faithful God who loves people and, even in his judgment, is long-suffering. The God who spoke the world into being could have spoken a boat into existence, sent a flood overnight, and wiped everyone out, but God didn't do that. He shows us countless details related to his patience and forbearance, even in the midst of judgment.

This account is a reminder that the God we serve is a faithful, longsuffering God who doesn't allow sin to go unpunished. Not only is God long-suffering but also he placed his faithful servant in full view, commanding him to build a boat (which took a long time to build) as a witness to a watching world of a God who rescues and a God who redeems. We are similarly called to be faithful, long-suffering witnesses to a watching world. We are called to love God and to tell others of God's redeeming love for them, which he has demonstrated by sending his Son.

To view the Scriptures this way requires a different way of seeing. It requires us to find our story in God's story. CliffsNotes don't help us see that. They give us information stripped of wonder and beauty. If we give our kids facts alone, they may be able to answer our questions, but will the story of God grip their hearts? When we see our story and God's story as separate from each other or we use God's story as an add-on to our story, we will misread and misapply the Bible in ways that distort and deform who God is and misshape our understanding of the focus and direction of redemptive history.

Eugene Peterson clearly explains the contrast between these two ways of reading in his book *Leap Over a Wall:*

> Somewhere along the way, most of us pick up bad habits of extracting from the Bible what we pretentiously call "spiritual principles," or "moral guidelines," or "theological truths," and then corseting ourselves in them in order to force a godly shape on our lives. That's a mighty uncomfortable way to go about improving our condition. And it's not the gospel way. *Story* is the gospel way. Story isn't imposed on our lives; it invites us into its life. As we enter and imaginatively participate, we find ourselves in a more spacious, freer, and more coherent world. . . . Story is the primary means we have for learning what the world is, and what it means to be a human being in it.[2]

Story is the gospel way. It is an invitation to a life that is real. This invitation doesn't come through the imposition of our way of seeing or being. It comes through total submission to God's way and learning how to see all of life as it was always meant to be.

THE PRINCIPLE: THE GOSPEL IS THE STORY OF ALL STORIES

We live in a culture that loves efficiency, so we settle for facts about people and things. Facts are efficient; stories are not.

Fingernails grow faster on the hand with which a person writes. On average, a person will blink approximately 4,200,000 times in a single year. By the time a person is seventy years old, he or she will have consumed over 12,000 gallons of water.

All these facts are true, but they don't tell you about what it means to be a human. Facts tell us what a human is. We need stories to convey what it is like to be a human. Facts engage our minds; stories grip our hearts and transform our minds.

Our story finds its meaning in the true story of how the world began, how we broke it, how Jesus came back to redeem it, and how one day he will make it the way it always was meant to be.

We see this narrative show up again and again in classic literature (and even modern movies), because our cultural history has been significantly shaped by scriptural themes, whether we automatically recognize it or not. I just say this from the perspective of someone who grew up outside of the US and outside of a Judeo-Christian culture, and I would be hesitant to say that every story in the world finds its story in God's story. Cinderella is one example, but when you look at the structure of most stories that have stood the test of time and resonate deeply with their audience, you will find that they follow this structure. J. R. R. Tolkien, in his epic article entitled *On Fairy Stories*, points to the reality that every fairy story has what he calls a "Eucatastrophe"—this inbreaking of joy in which every story finds its fulfillment, its happily-ever-after.

> It has long been my feeling (a joyous feeling) that God redeemed the corrupt making-creatures, men, in a way fitting to this aspect, as to others, of their strange nature. The Gospels contain a fairy-story, or a story of a larger kind which embraces all the

essence of fairy-stories. They contain many marvels—peculiarly artistic, beautiful, and moving: "mythical" in their perfect, self-contained significance; and among the marvels is the greatest and most complete conceivable Eucatastrophe. But this story has entered History and the primary world; the desire and aspiration of sub-creation has been raised to the fulfillment of Creation. The Birth of Christ is the Eucatastrophe of Man's history. The Resurrection is the Eucatastrophe of the story of the Incarnation. This story begins and ends in joy.[3]

"The Gospels contain a fairy-story, or a story of a larger kind which embraces all the essence of fairy-stories." Tolkien isn't saying the Gospels are made up. He is saying that understanding God's story makes every other story make sense. He is saying that every story arc points to the story of God. Regardless of the differences, these made-up stories find their source in God's story. The reason they resonate is because of the true story they emulate.

What Tolkien is saying is that every act of sub-creation, in which we make something from the materials created for us by God through the power of his Word, reflects Christ coming into our world—the incarnation—resulting in joy. The resurrection is the inbreaking of joy in the story of redemption. The incarnation and the resurrection are the inbreaking of God into our world, what Tolkien calls a "Eucatastrophe" that culminates in joy—happily ever after.

Abridged stories give us the facts. If you don't know the story for yourself, you will never see the beauty from facts alone. We understand the story God is writing through the inbreaking of Christ into our world and we understand the end of our story through the resurrection of Christ. To sum up: facts tell us who we are, but stories tell us whose we are.

Creation

There was nothing, and still, there was God, who is and has always been love since before time began. God, in his great love within himself, wanted to share that love, so he created everything out of nothing to live in love and for love, and the world he made was perfect.

He created all of creation and said it was good. He created men and women in his image and likeness and said that it was very good.

Humanity was given total freedom in the sinless created state, along with one command—to obey God—and they disobeyed. Milton famously said that the sin of disobedience "brought death into the world and all our woe."[4]

God created us and the world we live in out of grace and in love. It was out of the overflow of the love that God has within himself that he desired to create a world to share with us who he is and what he is like. Christopher Watkin brilliantly drives this point home—creation was an act of grace and love, not necessity.

> Neither we nor the universe are necessary. We may be important, precious, glorious, even, but we are precisely and gloriously unnecessary. This is the first instance of a figure (grace) that we will encounter many times on our journey through the Bible. Sometimes, we will encounter it as the figure of gratuity, at other times as the figure of superabundance. In a theological register, we might refer to it as grace, and we encounter this grace not first in redemption but in creation. It is through grace that the Christian is born again, but it is also through grace that the universe is born in the first place.[5]

God did not make the universe to satisfy something that was incomplete in him. He does not need the universe to be who he is, and he does not need us to be fulfilled.

As Paul stresses to the assembled Areopagus in Acts 17, "The God who made the world and everything in it, being Lord of heaven and earth, does not live in temples made by man, nor is he served by human hands, as though he needed anything, since he himself gives to all mankind life and breath and everything" (vv. 24–25).

Watkin continues:

> Creation-as-gift also tells us something about this universe in which we live precisely because it is needless; it puts us in a reality that is "an expression of a love always directed toward another," as well as an expression of God's delight in difference and proliferation. In short, the universe as such, by the mere fact of its existence, speaks of the glory and the love of God.[6]

Fall

In the biblical narrative, the fall represents a momentous event when humanity, driven by the desire to be like God, disobeyed his command and, in doing so, deviated from his intended plan, leading to a distortion and misrepresentation of God. This rebellion, initiated by the deceitful serpent's lies to Adam and Eve, introduced sin into our world. Its consequences extended far beyond the act of disobedience, resulting in relational separation from a holy God.

The problem at the heart of the human condition, whether it's the sinfulness of Adam and Eve or our own individual sins, is not a matter of degree. It's not about being mostly good or mostly bad. Even those who are considered genuinely good people have, at some point, transgressed God's commands and laws. The fundamental issue of our sin lies in the direction of our actions; we have sinned against God. This is a profound spiritual truth expressed in Psalm 51, where the psalmist acknowledges the deeply ingrained nature of human sinfulness.

The consequences of our sin are significant. We find ourselves forever separated from an eternally holy God. This separation is not merely a temporal or physical one but extends into the spiritual and eternal realm. The breach between humanity and God is not something that can be easily mended, as it is rooted in the fundamental problem of sin.

The fall serves as a critical backdrop to the overarching narrative of the Bible, setting the stage for the need for redemption and ultimately pointing toward the hope of restoration, in which the breach caused by sin is fully repaired, and humanity can once again be in perfect harmony with a holy God.

Redemption

Redemption stands as the cherished hope of every Christian. It is the aspiration that stirs within us once our eyes are opened to the world as God originally designed it, a world that has been marred and defaced by our own transgressions. This realization awakens a profound longing, a yearning for someone to come and restore what has been broken, both intentionally and inadvertently.

For those who are lost, redemption is like the sweet fragrance of a warm spring day. It carries the promise of life in every budding flower and every scent wafting through the gentle breeze. The concept of redemption is deeply rooted in the human experience, offering the prospect of renewal and a second chance, a chance to experience the world as it was meant to be.

Yet, for Christ, the very embodiment of perfection (as affirmed in Hebrews 4:15), the journey of redemption was an earth-shattering loss. It was a process that induced profound grief and overwhelming sorrow. The weight of bearing humanity's sin and brokenness, the cost of redemption, was a burden that only someone truly divine and truly human could shoulder.

George Herbert, in his poetic brilliance, captures the essence of redemption in his words:

> O all ye who pass by, behold and see;
> Man stole the fruit, but I must climb the tree;
> The tree of life for all, but only me:
> Was ever grief like mine?[7]

These lines poignantly convey the unique sacrifice and sorrow of Christ as he bore the sins of humanity, climbing the tree of crucifixion to bring life and redemption to all.

Redemption is not a free gift, for it came at a great cost to God. The idea of the sweet exchange emerges here. In this divine transaction, Christ offers his own perfection in place of our sin. Sin necessitates a payment, and Christ, as the Redeemer, pays that price with his own life. The broken relationship between God and humanity, severed by sin, requires mending. Only someone who is both truly God and truly man, like Christ, can fulfill this role. His dual nature, fully divine and fully human, uniquely qualifies him to bridge the gap and reconcile humanity with God. His death as a man, yet without sin due to his divinity, underscores the extraordinary nature of his role as the Redeemer, enabling us to find salvation and restoration in him in a way that no other can provide.

So, what can repair this breach? The solution to this profound dilemma lies in the concept of redemption. God, in his love and mercy, provided a way for reconciliation and salvation—through the life, death, and resurrection of Jesus Christ. Jesus is the ultimate bridge between humanity's sinful condition and God's holiness. Through faith in Christ and his atoning work, individuals can find forgiveness and restoration, mending the broken relationship with God. The final restoration of all things will happen when God comes to make all things new, fully and finally restoring all things to himself and bringing Christ's work of redemption to its final consummation. However, that process begins now in the personal lives of Christians as we obey the commands that God gives us in his Word and seek to influence culture for his glory.

There are many facts about God we can learn and should know, but what the human heart wants is a story. And by that, I don't mean a fictional story like Cinderella or even random Bible stories about animals. We want the whole story—a true story, a story that contains all other stories.

What pointed C. S. Lewis to Christ was his deep love for literature and stories. What led him to lasting faith was when he learned that the Christian story was true. Not only was it true but also it was the story that held every story. It was the story of God's love for us in Christ that held every page of our Scripture together. A holistic understanding of the Bible recognizes that it is supernaturally connected over centuries, telling one grand story that isn't about us (although it's for us). It's God's story about God.

The Practice: Tell All Stories for God's Glory

In every CliffsNotes book there are sections to make you familiar with what you didn't read. There is one section on the plot, another on key words, and still another naming all the characters in the story, usually in order of appearance. If you didn't read the book, you wouldn't know from the list alone who the main characters are and how they interact. I think this is a real danger for so many Christians discipled in this way; this can lead us to see characters and stories in a disconnected way; because we don't know how they relate to the grand story. This can also result in us overemphasizing our role and location in the story because we aren't able to see how every story points to Jesus and his redemptive work on our behalf. Our purpose is to give God the glory, and we, as a result, get the joy. The first question of the Westminster Catechism clarifies that our purpose is only found in God. The first question of the New City Catechism asks: "What is our only comfort in life and death? Answer: That I am not my own, but belong with body and soul, both in life and in death, to my faithful Savior Jesus Christ."[8] We are not the masters of our fate or the captains of our souls. We belong to God.

Connect every story to the bigger story of God

When he appeared to the disciples after he rose again on the road to Emmaus, Jesus told them about himself. The Bible says in Luke 24:27, "And beginning with Moses and all the Prophets, he interpreted to them in all the Scriptures the things concerning himself."

Jesus helped them see that every story in the Old Testament pointed forward to the Messiah. As we read the New Testament, the reference point for our hope is by looking back to the cross. When we realize that every page of the Old Testament is written in anticipation of Christ and every page in the New Testament is written in reference to Christ, that realization forces us to proclaim Christ. First Corinthians 2:1–2 states it this way: "And I, when I came to you, brothers, did not come proclaiming to you the testimony of

God with lofty speech or wisdom. For I decided to know nothing among you except Jesus Christ and him crucified."

Every story we tell fits into the redemptive narrative framework. Every story points us to the Creation, Fall, Redemption, and Restoration storyline. Every story reflects an aspect of this overarching narrative that helps us understand the purpose of the Scriptures and facilitates their work in us.

How do I teach this passage in a distinctively Christian way?[9]

This question is beneficial to ask when teaching Old Testament narratives. Non-Christian historians can teach these stories with cultural accuracy, and Jewish rabbis can speak of God's mighty acts within the narratives. However, both lack a Christ-centered lens through which to interpret and teach these passages.

Consider the story of Daniel and the lions' den. Teachers can read and describe the details of this story perfectly. They can speak of Daniel's exemplary character and even of the unique way God saves Daniel in his time of need, and while there is nothing wrong with these facts of the story, they're insufficient on their own. To teach the story fully, leaders need to tell the story in a uniquely Christian way. How? First, the point of the story isn't to be like Daniel. The point of the story is to reveal God. Second, as Christians, we can ask, "How does this story reveal God *in Christ*?" After King Darius learns that no harm has come to Daniel, he decrees that everyone should fear the God of Daniel, who delivered him from the lions and saved his life (Daniel 6:26–27). Does God still deliver and save today? Yes! We may not be trapped in a den of lions, but all people are bound by sin, and we Christians are bound by sin if we engage in it (Romans 6:16). We need Jesus to save us from the bondage of sin and shut the accusing mouth of Satan, who preys on us like a lion (1 Peter 5:8).

This question can also help us avoid moralism when teaching New Testament passages. The fruit of the Spirit is a favorite among teachers and kids, but it's easy to emphasize the fruit to the neglect of the Spirit. The point of Galatians 5:22–25 isn't to push believers to pull themselves up by their bootstraps and be more loving, joyful, peaceful, etc. The Spirit indwells believers and will have specific characteristics, or fruit, spring up in those who walk in step with him. For instance, love is said to be a fruit of living in step with the Spirit, but are Christians always loving? Of course not. We get angry, hold grudges, and are inclined to hate our enemies. Has anyone ever loved perfectly? Yes! Jesus demonstrated perfect love by dying for us while we were still sinners (Romans 5:8). Christ perfectly embodies and displays each fruit. If we want our kids to understand the fruit of the Spirit, then we need to show them that only lives rooted in Christ will result in this type of fruit.

Which aspect of the gospel is shown in this story?[10]

As you walk through a biblical narrative, it's helpful to read it with the main aspects or movements of the gospel in mind. How does the framework of creation impact the story you are teaching? What conditions of the fall come to the surface? Is redemption displayed, and how does Christ accomplish the same thing but better? Was anything restored in the story, and how does that foreshadow the ultimate Restoration to come?

The book of Nehemiah is often referenced for its insights and principles on leadership. Such principles may exist within his story, but the book's primary purpose is not to communicate those principles. Nehemiah wasn't written to teach us how to be good leaders, but it was written to show us how God is faithful to keep his promises. After Israel had been taken captive, God made a promise to Jeremiah that he would liberate them and restore what was destroyed. Throughout the books of Ezra and Nehemiah, we see God keep his promise to restore the people, the temple, and the walls of the city. What aspect of the grand narrative of the gospel is seen in this story? Restoration! If God is faithful to keep his promise to restore Israel in their time of captivity, then we can trust that he will keep his promise to restore creation and make all things new. Nehemiah points to the good news that all things will be made new because of the life, death, resurrection, and return of Christ.

How does God accomplish the same thing—only better—in Jesus?[11]

We slipped this question in earlier but wanted to pose it more explicitly here. Throughout Scripture, we see God's people do extraordinary things. Take Esther, for example. She stood on behalf of her people, knowing it could lead to death. The story is gripping and incredibly inspiring. Is there a point in Scripture where God accomplishes the same thing, but better, in Christ? You'd better believe it! Christ stood on our behalf, knowing that he would be put to death for our sins. Esther may have stood on behalf of her people, but Jesus died on behalf of his enemies (Romans 5). Jesus is better than Esther! We glorify God when we make much of Christ in the stories we tell of his people.

Who in this story needs the good news?[12]

Everyone needs Jesus, even the heroes of the faith! It's easy to look at the extraordinary faith of men like Abraham and put them on a pedestal, but they also need Jesus's grace. Abraham may have trusted God with the life of his only son, Isaac, but he didn't always exercise perfect faith. Instead of trusting God to protect his wife when going to Egypt, Abraham lied to Pharaoh. Specifically, Abraham claimed that his wife was his sister (Genesis 12:10–20). Pharaoh experienced the consequences of this lie and eventually sent Abraham and Sarah away.

Who needs the good news of Jesus in this story? Abraham. He didn't trust God and tried to take matters into his own hands. He needs Jesus, the One who always speaks truth and entrusted his life to his faithful Father in the midst of his suffering (1 Peter 2:23). Our kids need this good news as well.

From this example, we see how the right questions can build bridges to the best conclusions. At the end of each story, children should see Christ and understand the story in light of his glorious gospel. This, however, does not mean that Christ is behind every nook and cranny of a biblical passage. In our right desire to point to Christ in all of Scripture, we must be cautious of forcing a connection to Christ where there is none. For example, just because David uses a stone to kill the giant and Jesus is later described as the chief cornerstone doesn't mean that the stone slung by David represents Christ. This extreme form of allegory can turn any moment, person, or object into a symbol of Christ, which can twist Scripture in unhelpful, manipulative, and dangerous ways. Prayerfully work through the questions above, read correlating passages and commentaries, and seek guidance from your pastors as you prepare to make much of Christ in all of Scripture.

Teach all the stories of the Bible, even the difficult stories

If we teach a CliffsNotes version of the Bible, our kids will know all the main points of the Bible but will not be able to connect those dots because they are facts for their consumption rather than a story of their redemption. One of the reasons kids don't understand the gospel is because we edit stories that we think are too difficult for them to hear. We give them the highlights and wonder why they don't understand the beauty of the gospel as they grow. Kids are not stupid; they know real evil exists and that injustice is alive today. If we do not tell the stories of the Bible that address real evil and the injustice of our world, our kids will dismiss the Bible as irrelevant.

If we believe that every story in the Bible is given to us for our edification and growth in godliness, we have to stop asking *which* stories we should teach our kids, and we need to start asking *how* we teach each story to our kids. We need to help point them to Jesus, especially in the hard stories.

Finally, we need to tell every story because faith in Jesus grows when we see what horrors he rescues us from. Author Jack Klumpenhower, in a guest post on my blog, explains that it is often the difficult stories, told in a way that helps kids see the beauty of God's power to save, that prove to be so invaluable. The faith of our kids grows deeper from robust stories of rescue, not oversimplified facts presented in CliffsNote form. Jack says this:

> It isn't enough for kids simply to be told Jesus saves them in some generic way. Many of them have already experienced betrayal, death, and other great evils—and if they haven't, they soon will. When this happens, we want them to turn to God because they've learned from a young age how God is faithful and good, especially in the midst of such horrors. Sadly, many people instead turn away from God at such times because sugarcoated stories about him are all they know.[13]

I could not agree more with what Jack is saying. As a kids' pastor for over twenty-five years, I have seen this to be true in far too many churches. I love how Question 15 of the New City Catechism frames the purpose of the law of God in our lives. The question is this: "Since no one can keep the law, what is its purpose?" The answer is this: "That we may know the holy nature and will of God, and the sinful nature and disobedience of our hearts; and thus our need of a Savior."[14]

Do not skip the hard stories of the Bible, or your kids will never see this purpose. They will, instead, believe they are basically good and God is a superstition rather than a Savior. What is the purpose of every story? To show us God's perfection in Christ, the sinfulness of our hearts, and how much we need God's help. Every kid needs this.

Spend time preparing Bible stories to glorify God

Preaching the hard stories of the Bible takes preparation. You cannot walk into class and preach to kids in a way that is age appropriate and has proper application without preparation. This requires that we look for curricula that address these stories. It requires that we train our leaders and teams to know how to address difficult issues and see the gospel in all of Scripture.

We live in a time of profound disorientation. Our kids need solid truth and gospel hope. We can provide this in our messages to kids, filling them with confidence that comes from looking backward to the cross. It is essential to remind kids that we can have confidence in a world that is shaking—not because we are good, but because we belong to God.

Our preaching to kids must also contain the present assurance that God is with us—that even though Jesus left the earth, he sent us his Spirit to help us (John 14:16), guide us (John 16:13), and be with us until the end of the age (Matthew 28:20). Finally, we must tell our kids of the future hope we have, knowing that even in the brokenness we see around us, we have a certain hope that God is coming back to make all things new (Revelation 21:5).

But rather than orienting ourselves to the gospel, the temptation in teaching children is to fall into moralizing. We tend to focus, by default, on how the story shows us how to behave, rather than emphasizing how it orients our hearts to the story of the gospel. But this is what our kids need: a way of seeing the gospel shape of every story as it tells the ultimate story of God's redeeming love.

We must understand the framework of the gospel message and not move on from that to something new. God created a perfect world; in sin, we broke that world. God, in his mercy, sent Jesus to redeem our world and will one day come back to make our world the way it was always supposed to be. We must teach this to our kids. It is the story of God for us in one sentence. This is something we proclaim to them so that they will clearly see it proclaimed in Scripture, and so that they will proclaim it to a world that is devoid of hope and truth.

Christ's last command to us needs to be the focus of what we do. We are not called to entertain but to engage kids. We are not called to pacify but to proclaim; we are not called to babysit but to make disciples. Matthew 28:18–20 says,

> And Jesus came and said to them, "All authority in heaven and on earth has been given to me. Go therefore and make disciples of all nations, baptizing them in the name of the Father and of the Son and of the Holy Spirit, teaching them to observe all that I have commanded you. And behold, I am with you always, to the end of the age."

From this passage, we must remember that we go in the authority that is given, not in any authority of our own. Our priority is not to teach kids the basics of the Bible stories, but to make disciples. Our teaching is not about what we think, but what Christ has taught us in his Scripture. And we go to do this work knowing that we are not alone and that God is with us.

We are gospel people. We are called to disciple our kids in these precious truths. This could seem overwhelming, and, at many times, it may be. But rest in this, dear worker and fellow believer: this glorious task to which we are called is not one we do alone. God has promised us that as we go and as we disciple and as we proclaim, he is with us until the end of the age. What a promise. What a comfort. What a Savior.

DISCUSSION QUESTIONS

1. In high school, did you read full-length books or did you read the CliffsNotes versions?

2. Why does the author suggest that stories are more valuable than simple facts or notes about stories? How does this idea relate to the Bible's role in our understanding of God?

3. What is "CliffsNotes Christianity," and why does the author argue that it's a problem? How can we avoid falling into this way of understanding the Bible?

4. How will seeing the stories in Scripture through the framework of Creation, Fall, Redemption, and Restoration change the way you communicate truth?

5. Why is it important not to skip the "hard stories" of the Bible, especially when teaching them to children? How can we ensure that kids understand the deeper, redemptive aspects of these stories rather than just glean moral lessons?

Chapter 5

Simplifying vs. Distilling Theology

Most days in your high school career are less than memorable. Fewer still are shared experiences that bond generations of Americans together. But what nearly all American kids have experienced is dissection day in their high school science class. When you dissect small animals, you discover who the doctors are in a second. You don't forget the sights, sounds, and smells. I (Sam) remember those days in the science lab as if they were yesterday. I remember several kids screaming, a few almost fainting, and a couple more excited than they should have been. The rest of us experienced a mixture of fear, excitement, and nervousness.

In addition to frog dissection, we also learned about elements and lit some things on fire, but I'll never forget two concepts I learned that year from my AP science class: simplification and distillation. Both are much less traumatic than formaldehyde frogs. Simplification is the reduction of a substance to its most basic version. When you simplify a task, rule, or substance, you are fighting to remove as much complexity as possible to get down to the fewest possible parts or requirements. Distillation is the removal of elements in a liquid through the application of heat. For example in the case of seawater, it would be sodium and chlorine that are distilled out because NaCl (standard salt) is removed. It is the separation of elements that were previously in a mixture.

When you distill, you keep the essentials and remove the unnecessary things. In simplification, you remove anything that is difficult or complex, and you even, at times, remove what is essential. Simplification waters down the truth; distillation elevates it.

The Problem: Simplifying the Truth

For the first ten years that I served my church as a children's pastor, I thought my job was to be the CSO: the chief simplification officer. I looked at theology as complex and children as unable to grasp complex thinking and sought to simplify both theology and the Bible for the kids I was called to serve. I thought it was my job to determine what Bible stories should be taught and what truths about God kids could understand. I thought it was my job to reduce mysteries that the church has wrestled with for centuries into memorable catchphrases for kids to consume and easily digest. The problem with simplification is that deep truths and complex ideas are so entrenched in the stories of Scripture that we remove essential truths in our desire to create consumable faith.

The problem isn't in our right desire to apply truth to kids in a way they can hear, understand, and apply. It is in the kind of questions we are asking. When our goal is simplification, we ask, "What parts of the Bible are applicable to kids?" Those who are distillers of truth ask a different question. They ask, "How can I teach all of Scripture to the kids God has charged me to shepherd?"

Simplification asks, "What can I teach?" Distillation asks, "How can I teach this?" Distillation is the process by which we take a passage of Scripture or Bible story, which can be complex, and apply the heat of the Spirit of God through prayer and study, through which the Spirit guides us into truth. The result is concentration of truth and clarity as we come to see the truth. There are parts of Scripture that are complex and even difficult; the goal of distillation of truth is not to ignore difficult passages like simplification can often do. The goal of distillation is to focus on the message of the text and what the passage meant to those to whom it was written and then to convey that truth in an age-appropriate way to the kids you are teaching.

Simplification and distillation are not just scientific terms; they have real-life consequences. Growing up, we didn't have a lot of money, so soda was not our family's guilty pleasure. We instead bought packets of Kool-Aid. It was far cheaper but delivered the much-needed sugar rush that kids crave and mothers fear. Who doesn't love Kool-Aid?

As a kid, few characters in commercials on TV grabbed my attention like the giant pitcher of Kool-Aid, appropriately named "Kool-Aid." The kids in school would call his name, "Hey Kool-Aid," and he would burst through the walls. I would beg my mom daily for Kool-Aid, and on rare occasions, I would convince her to buy a small paper package of concentrated goodness. I would rush into the house with the now-wrinkled package of Kool-Aid that my death grip created, so excited for my mom to make the red mustache-inducing liquid that hydrated me as a child. Even though we didn't have a lot of money, my mom did two things right: she added lots of sugar and not much water. The result was a six-year-old's version of sugar water red dye moonshine.

I had no idea our Kool-Aid was strong until I went to a friend's house. My friend's mom was concerned about sugar content and dyes, so she added so much water to the mix that the result was unrecognizable. Needless to say, the light-pink, watered-down version did not pack the kind of punch that would make a glass jug of red deliciousness break through a brick wall. I wanted Kool-Aid, and my friend's mom gave us awful water.

Simplification in theology adds what is unnecessary and removes essential elements to make sure what you are teaching is understandable. You avoid telling stories that involve death, sorrow, sin, and difficulty. You talk a lot about God's love without the context of the need for that love and the uniqueness of that love.

> When we add so much water to our stories about God, we produce a faith that is not grounded in Scripture but based on our understanding of love. We produce a faith that is tame.

We produce a faith that our kids will grow out of because it is not strong enough to handle the difficulties that they will face in this life because of a fallen world and fallen man.

When you simplify something in science or in nature, you add stuff to dilute whatever you are simplifying. You pour water into a concentrated drink to dilute and simplify. The result is a watered-down product. When you distill something, you cook out what is not essential and leave only the things that are heavy in a smaller, more concentrated form. When we ask what stories or doctrines kids should be taught, we skip troublesome stories or deep topics because those stories or topics might be too much for kids to handle.

THE PRINCIPLE: DISTILLING THE TRUTH

Several years ago, we had to teach a passage of Scripture where God rescued Israel from slavery in Egypt. The simple thing would have been to skip that story because stories about dying kids may not work well for first graders. But we become distillers of truth, as we should be, when we stop and ask, "How should I teach this lesson?"

What is true about the story of the death angel killing the firstborn boy of every home that did not have the blood of a lamb? It shows us God's justice and mercy. That story shows God's ability to save those who belong to him. That story shows the hero of the exodus is not Moses but God. When we simplify the story, we make Moses the hero and tell our kids to be bold and strong like Moses. The message is different if we tell our kids the God we serve is filled with justice and mercy, that he saves us when we are powerless to save ourselves, that he gave us his Son, and that he saved us at the cost of his firstborn Son's life. Now we are distilling the truth.

What does distillation look like? In our children's ministry, one of our leaders teaching this lesson told our kids of God's power to save those who are his. This leader told about the justice and mercy of God in this story, about an innocent lamb that was killed, and about how the blood of the lamb was applied to the door of the home. Every home that had the blood of an innocent lamb was safe. For kids, this story can be scary. There are few things more frightening than the thought of a spiritual being (someone who can't be touched, seen, heard, or fought—in this case, the death angel) coming at night and killing kids. That doesn't mean you skip this story. In fact, you have to teach this story to kids because of the implications of it and how it so blatantly points to Christ. The question is not if we should teach it, but how can we help kids feel the weight, get the point, and, as a result of hearing this story, worship Christ for all he has done.

Here is how we told it: As the storyteller was relating the events of the Exodus, small group leaders took a two-inch red ribbon and crisscrossed it over the heads of the kids. The ribbon wasn't over the head of every kid. The storyteller got to the end of the story and explained that God sent an angel of death to kill every firstborn son in Egypt, but those who had the blood of an innocent lamb were safe. The storyteller then said to look above your head, and if there is a ribbon above you, grab it with your right hand. The kids reached up to grab hold of the ribbon that had been provided. The storyteller ended by saying the children of Israel were saved by God's mercy. We, too, are saved by God's mercy. Everyone who puts their faith in Jesus, the Lamb of God who died instead of us, will be saved. That, my friends, is distillation—using understandable language and vivid illustrations to teach the point of the text.

My seminary professor would often tell us that in preaching the point of the text should be the point of our sermon. In distillation, we don't include every detail of the passage, but we make sure that the focus of our message to our kids reflects the message of the passage in particular and the message of all of Scripture in general. When we simplify truth, we add what we shouldn't add and remove what we shouldn't remove. The result is a one-dimensional vision of a multifaceted God. When we tell the hard stories and the difficult ones, our kids will understand that God is not a God we control, and sometimes, our kids won't be able to understand fully. They will, however, grow into an understanding of a powerful, gracious, loving, and holy God that loves us more than we could ever know.

This is the danger of simplifying faith. We try to make it so accessible and safe that we inadvertently inoculate our kids from faith. They get just enough of God that when life hurts, our kids apply what they learned about God, but it isn't a robust, powerful, unsafe, good faith that they apply. The simple faith they grew up in isn't powerful enough for the deep sorrows and dark nights. They tried faith, and it didn't work.

When our primary concern is to make faith simple, fun, and accessible, we modernize stories in ways that obscure the meaning. When the goal is fun, we add silly things that sometimes change the story. Imagine us telling the story of the death angel in Egypt, and instead, we make it about Darth Vader and Luke because kids like *Star Wars*. Another more subtle example would be in the stories of Jonah and Noah. Often, the focal points in many lessons I have seen are on the fish portion of Jonah and the boat part of Noah (which is actually an extremely minor part of the narrative), and they neglect the gritty details of each of those stories. The story of Jonah, in particular, is all about Jonah calling God's wisdom and mercy into question. Jonah knows God is merciful, but questions whether he deals out his mercy wisely/correctly. Like in Genesis, we see God as a God who is both gracious and just in his dealings with mankind. These stories are designed to make readers evaluate their own understanding of who God saves and how God saves. In our right desire to make the truth engaging, we end up giving our kids Flavor-Aid instead of Kool-Aid. We simplify through our extreme focus on relevance at the expense of the truth.

For far too long the church and parents have been guilty of trying to make Christ more attractive by adding ideas and extra biblical content to the gospel to make it more appealing. In doing this, we have robbed the gospel of its power. When we distill truth, we set aside the details that are good (but can sometimes distract from the point of the text) and leave behind the powerful core of the truth for children to understand. Jesus taught in a way a child would understand; why shouldn't we?

It is far easier to simplify truth, but distilling it is much more effective. Distillation is so powerful because you are not giving your kids a faith that they will grow out of . . . you are giving your kids a faith they will grow into. When you distill truth, you refuse to compromise the truth and seek to answer the question: How will I help my kids understand what God has shown me and what he is like from his Word? When you distill truth, you create categories in the mind of your kids that they will need when they get older.

We need to do this for them when they come to us after church or when they are in a small group and ask deep questions—because they will. When they ask questions like, "What is faith?" will you be taken off guard and say, "It's when you believe something"? Did that answer the question? Sort of. It simplified the concept. Simplification often cuts concepts our culture would find offensive—such as sin, hell, and the exclusivity of faith—out of the Bible and out of our lessons. It also frames truth in a way that is not focused on what is biblically true but rather what is least offensive to others. Rewind to the conversation about faith from before and see the truth distilled. "What is faith?" You can tell the kids in your ministry that faith is all about trust. It is about putting our confidence in what Christ has done to rescue us, not in what we can do to regain God's favor and be restored to a proper relationship with him. It is understanding what the Bible says about who Jesus is and trusting him no matter what happens in life.

If you are asking, "How do we become distillers of truth and not simplifiers of it? How do I do this?" Well, distilling truth is not a reflex; it's a muscle we grow.

THE PRACTICE: DISTILL TRUTH

To illustrate the difference between simplification and distillation when it comes to truth, let's look at the doctrine of sin.

Simplification of the doctrine of sin

For example, when we simplify the doctrine of sin, we might say something like "Sin is doing wrong things. It is missing the mark, and sin hurts you and causes pain and sorrow in your life."

In our desire to apply the truth, we often take biblical truths and minimize their impact by doing two things:

1. We remove truths from their context: "Sin is doing wrong things." What wrong things? Wrong things defined by whom?
2. We jump to the application too soon. We talk about the effects of sin on us and make the message of the truth we are discussing overly individualistic and generic. Sin can only be rightly understood when we talk about the origin, the consequence, and the cure.

Distillation of the doctrine of sin

When talking to kids, they must understand that sin is a particular thing. The Westminster Confession states, "Every sin, both original and actual, being a transgression of the righteous law of God."[1] For kids to understand sin, we must establish the basis for our understanding in Scripture. We have to show that sin is not something that happens to us; it is something that we are born into.

Because we are descended from Adam and Eve, who were our first parents and our first representatives before God, we received the consequence of their sin and the same nature and ability to commit sins of our own. As a result, we sin and break God's laws daily on purpose and on accident. The question regarding our sin is, "What do kids need to know about sin?" I believe they need to know three things:

1. The nature of our sin and the greatness of our sin.
2. The nature of our forgiveness and help.
3. The response of gratitude that should come naturally from someone who has received forgiveness and has found life and joy in Christ.

There is much more to be said about sin, but for the sake of helping our kids remember and apply the truths we teach, you have to decide what to focus on, what to leave in, and what to leave for later. In the Bible and throughout church history, we see sin as ignoring God, rejecting God, or breaking his law. The three things articulated above are taken from a systematic approach to understanding sin but applied in a distilled manner. Is there more to know about sin? Yes, but the essential truths of sin that have to be upheld are these three, and they are the foundational structure for every catechism. Guilt of our sin, grace found in God's forgiveness in Christ, and gratitude, our response for so great a salvation.

What to say to kids about sin

The question we must ask is, How do we become better distillers through the process of applying principles of truth to any doctrine or text we encounter? The ability to know what is essential is not a by-product of personal or cultural preference. If reflecting personal or cultural preference were the goal, we would explicitly or implicitly distort the truth to reflect what we would prefer the text to say rather than faithfully represent what it does say. How do we faithfully represent what the text says with any doctrine or text we encounter? I would argue we do that through making God's Word foundational, historical theology formational, and our experience supplemental.

First, we start with the Word of God. We live in a postmodern, arguably post-Christian culture, and truth is considered to be whatever any one person believes truth to be. To be a follower of Christ, you have to start with the foundational understanding that the Scriptures are our source for truth, not your (or our) feelings. This is why, in every systematic theology book, the first doctrine we study is the Word of God. Without that as our source, nothing will make sense. The way we answered sin above was founded on Scripture.

Second, historical theology must be formational. By historical theology, I am referring to how the church throughout history has understood, applied, and explained Scripture. This is not only a collection of facts but also a rich tapestry of wisdom and insight that has been passed down to us. It is the counsel of many, many men and women who have given us truth that can be verified and filtered through the lens of Scripture. The primary sources that are helpful for us in teaching kids are biblical theology, systematic theology, covenantal theology, and catechisms. All these resources are condensed and systematized summaries of truths from Scripture. These summaries are important because the Word of God is not an afterthought or subservient to our ideas but is foundational to every thought, word, and deed.

Biblical theology gives you an understanding of every story and passage of Scripture in light of its place within the grand narrative of Scripture. It answers the question, "How does this passage point to and illustrate the creative purpose of God, the sinful nature of man, the redemptive work of God, and the restorative trajectory of God, who makes all things new?"

A systematic theology is a clarified explanation of theological topics that are categorized and systematized for you. It is written by scholars who spent (or have spent) their whole lives taking all of what the Scripture says about every theological topic and placing it in categories that we can easily access and apply in our teaching.

Covenantal theology helps us understand how God relates to us and how we are to relate to him. It shows us how, over time, God has revealed himself in such a way that we see the fullness of God in Christ. Each covenant between God and man pointed to the fuller and ultimate expression of God in Christ through the new covenant.

Catechisms provide a clarified understanding of core truths and a method for committing those truths to memory. They are great examples of distilled truth. They take complex doctrines covered in many pages in a systematic theology book and distill them down to several sentences.

Finally, our experience. Experience is vital to bringing these doctrinal truths to light. When we understand what Scripture says and what has been believed by those who have come before us, we can bring our experience to bear. However, our experience must always be subservient to Scripture and can only be rightly understood by the light of Scripture. We never place our experience above God's Word. If we don't understand something, then the problem isn't God's Word; it's our understanding and experience. For instance, if we have experienced sorrow and loss, that experience doesn't mean God is not good. It means we cannot see or understand at that moment the way God's goodness is meant for us. Scripture serves as a compass, guiding us through the complexities of our experiences and helping us to see them in the light of God's truth. [To see this explanation in a complete lesson, please see Appendix 2 at the back of the book.]

Using the tools mentioned above, if I were teaching kids about the doctrine of sin from a biblical passage or story, I would say something like this: "Kids, today we talked about sin. Sin is breaking God's laws and commands on purpose and by accident" (catechesis). "We talked about how we are born with a sinful nature and a desire to sin" (systematic theology). "We have done things that we know are wrong. Because we are sinful and God is holy," (systematic theology) "we are separated from God" (biblical theology). "But God, for all who trust in him alone, fixed our sin forever" (covenantal theology). "He, in love and mercy, sent Jesus," (biblical theology) "who lived a perfect life to take your punishment" (covenantal theology). "And because of Jesus, we are forgiven" (biblical theology) "and have been given this gift. We are thankful. Because we have been forgiven by God, we belong to Jesus, not to ourselves" (catechesis). "Because our guilt and sin have been forgiven and God's grace and mercy have been given to us, we live lives of thankfulness and gratitude" (catechesis). "Our lives are marked by guilt, grace, and gratitude."

Training leaders to distill truth

We all need training to learn how to distill truth. The reflexive reaction most of us have is not distillation, but simplification. In our right desire to help our kids understand biblical truth, we often overreach and remove the essential aspects that are formational and foundational to our faith.

Here are some ideas for how to help make distillation reflexive:

Ask God for wisdom

The Bible tells us that if we lack wisdom, we are to ask. One of the challenging aspects of teaching kids is that they ask questions that are difficult to explain. In some cases, they may ask questions for which we don't know the answers. Even when you do know the answers, it takes wisdom from God and his Word to understand what is being asked and to know how to apply the right answer in a way that helps our kids understand God's truth.

John Newton, the famous pastor and hymn writer, used a helpful analogy to explain the connection between the Word and prayer: "The chief means for attaining wisdom, and suitable gifts for the ministry, are the holy Scriptures and prayer. One is the fountain of living water, the other the bucket with which we are to draw."[2]

There have been times in my life when I haven't known what to pray, and I have a couple of practices that have been helpful in these situations. The first is to pray Scripture. Find a psalm or passage of Scripture and incorporate that into a prayer. For example, James 1:5 states, "If any of you lacks wisdom, let him ask God, who gives generously to all without reproach, and it will be given him."

You could turn that into a prayer by saying, "Lord, you say in your Word that if we lack wisdom, we are to ask. God, right now, I ask for wisdom in leading this group of kids so that my words would reflect your heart. Lord, I thank you for being generous with us when we come to you. Help me to be generous to all who come to me. And finally, I thank you for the assurance I have from your Word that you will do what you promise. I need your wisdom and grace to lead kids in such a way that they find you beautiful, not me brilliant."

Another great help for me in my times of prayer has been reading and praying the prayers of faithful Christians who have gone before me. One classic example of prayers that others have prayed that are an example to us and a source of life for us is Arthur Bennett's collection of Puritan prayers in his book *The Valley of Vision*. If you are looking for a more modern example, I would recommend *Every Moment Holy* by Douglas Kaine McKelvey and Ned Bustard, and Johnathan Gibson's *Be Thou My Vision*.

Anticipate the questions kids will ask

Through the crucible of pastoring and parenting, I have come to find that all kids want to know the answers to basic questions. The goal of this book is to get you to think and prepare for the times when your kids ask you to give a reason for the hope that is in you (1 Peter 3:15).

There are a few practices you need to have in place that will prepare you to be ready for your interactions with kids. Many of you might think there is no way you could teach your kids theology because you don't understand it yourself. Take heart. You are not alone. The good news for you is that many resources are now available to help you (and your kids) understand the basic framework of our faith.

Theology is scary for many parents and leaders alike, as many of them were never intentionally taught theology because much of it was assumed when they were kids. Their parents assumed they understood things about God. The most important thing about our kids is what they think about God. Because that's true, we can leave nothing to chance.

To do that, I would recommend the following books:

- For teaching kids 3–5
  Everything a Child Should Know About God by Kenneth Taylor (10Publishing, 2014)
- For teaching kids 5–9
  The Ology: Ancient Truths Ever New by Marty Machowski (New Growth Press, 2015)
- For teaching kids 9–13
  Big Truths for Young Hearts: Teaching and Learning the Greatness of God by Bruce Ware (Crossway, 2009)
- For teaching kids 13–18
  Christian Beliefs: Twenty Questions Every Christian Should Know by Wayne Grudem (Zondervan Academic, 2022)

The more you understand your faith, the easier it will be for you to explain it to the children you teach. The brilliant and famous theologian Dietrich Bonhoeffer often said, "If one couldn't communicate the most profound ideas about God and the Bible to children, something was amiss. There was more to life than academia."[3]

One final thought is that you need to prepare your heart as well as your mind. To prepare your heart, I would offer two simple suggestions:

1. Make a consistent time of prayer and reading God's Word a lifelong habit.
2. Make the reading of poetry a lifelong challenge. Poetry combines efficiency in word use with beauty

in prose in a powerful way that is life-giving to you and those you lead. Two poets who were pastoral in their approach and are helpful to any Christian are John Donne and George Herbert.

Understand the gospel enough to be able to point our kids continually back to Christ

You do not have to be a biblical scholar, but you do have to read your Bible. When your back is pinned to the wall by four-year-olds wanting answers about the everlasting states of their pet frogs, what is in you is going to come out. Don't give them simple pat answers. Give them Jesus. Give them distilled truth.

There are not a lot of books on this topic, but I will point you in two directions—one is a practice, and the other is a resource.

The practice: come prepared. When you know what you are talking about that week and have spent thirty minutes to an hour studying and meditating on the Word of God and the content you will be sharing in a large group or small group, you will be more ready for the questions that will come your way. When you are talking about Cain and Abel, you need to be ready to answer questions about anger, murder, and dysfunction in families. If you are not ready and haven't thought through the implications of your lesson and how the gospel comes to bear on each aspect, you will probably give your kids a pat answer.

What is a pat answer? It is an overly simplistic answer that gets you off the hot seat. It answers the question on a basic level but doesn't point kids back to Jesus. Pat answers are often half-truths or soft truths that distort or obscure the truth. I remember a lesson that I looked over one year for Easter. The lesson written for our preschool-age children was around the death and resurrection of Jesus—not a simple topic, but so important to get right. The curriculum whiffed because it told us to tell the preschoolers that Jesus "Went away and came back." We didn't teach that. A pat answer gives kids enough information to solve their curiosity but not enough information to instill wonder.

It is also helpful to remember to be humble enough to admit that we don't have all the answers. We need to be comfortable with telling kids, "That's a good question, and it deserves a good answer. Let me think and read and pray about it and get back to you in a few weeks." Then follow through and learn what you need to know to give that kid (and the others present) a robust, theologically accurate answer.

When you, as the leader, are prepared, you model preparation to the other leaders and create a place where questions can be asked and where our answers point kids to Jesus.

Second, a resource: I would encourage you to get the book *Show Them Jesus* by Jack Klumpenhower (New Growth Press, 2014). In this book, Jack, who is a volunteer teacher at his church, does a masterful job showing you practical ways to point kids to Jesus in your teaching time. I interviewed Jack on my blog and asked him about questions kids have and how to teach hard stories in the Bible. Jack said:

> Faith in Jesus grows when we see what horrors he rescues us from. It isn't enough for kids simply to be told Jesus saves them in some generic way. . . . If you teach Bible stories to kids you will still have to decide for yourself how much they can handle and understand. Much depends on the specific kids, so I can't tell you exactly what to do. But I will say that when you teach the Bible the way it's given, acknowledging the evil of the world and tracing a path to the love of Jesus, you give kids the one lesson they most need to hear for all of life. Don't be too quick to skip those disturbing stories.[4]

Amen, Jack. This kind of understanding of God and his ways comes from personal study of Scripture, intentional lesson preparation, and a commitment to gospel application.

Ask someone who is smarter than you

I remember watching *Who Wants to Be a Millionaire* for the first time. I got all the questions right until a certain point. I thought I could dominate, then I hit a wall right around the same time the contestant did. Then something amazing happened. Regis told her she could "phone a friend." I didn't even flinch. I knew exactly who I would call—my good friend Rick, who is way smarter than I. I knew then what I know now: I could win *Who Wants to Be a Millionaire* because of my average intelligence combined with my friend Rick's superior intellect. It was right at that moment that I had a God thought. If I would feel comfortable calling my friend Rick about who was the heaviest president based on the percentage of body weight, then why would I not call him about stuff that really matters? We all have people in our lives that know more than we do. Call them and leverage their wisdom to help you distill the truth for your kids.

Here are some ideas for great ways to ask someone smarter than you:

1. Find a mentor who has been doing kid's ministry for longer than you and meet regularly for coffee or over Zoom.
2. Ask good questions on kids' ministry Facebook groups. There are several out there.
3. Network during kids' ministry conferences.
4. If you are part of a denomination, many have a kid's ministry specialist they employ to help you.
5. Email us. We may not be smarter than you, but we can find someone who is.

When you distill truth and avoid simplifying, you put suitcase handles to your kids' faith, and they can take it with them wherever they go. Distilled truth is not tame truth. It is a violent, life-transforming, never-be-the-same-again kind of truth. When you distill truth in a way that takes a complex idea, breaks it down, yet keeps the power of that truth intact, it's unforgettable. The reason it's unforgettable is that it elevates Christ. In distilling truth, we want to explain the truth to our kids in such a manner that they walk away in awe at the greatness of who Jesus is. I think we settle for simple truth because it's easier at the time, and the result is that our kids walk away thinking we are the smartest person they know. I never want my kids to marvel at my wisdom. I want them to stand in awe at the greatness of our Creator daily. I want Jesus to be the hero in every moment, in every story, and in every day. We simplify truth because we misunderstand our role in our kids' lives and our role in the lives of the kids to whom we minister. We think we are supposed to be their saviors. We are not. God has called us to be voices crying in the wilderness, telling our kids to prepare the way of the Lord. We are not supposed to be their saviors, just a signpost pointing to their Savior. When you distill truth, you do just that—you point your kids to a God who is completely unsafe but totally good.

Discussion Questions

1. Can you identify ways that you have been guilty of simplification in your teaching to kids? What are some examples where you have distilled truth in your ministry to kids?

2. How did the author initially approach teaching theology to children? What were the limitations of this approach?

3. In what ways does simplification potentially dilute the depth of faith in children, according to the chapter?

4. Give an example of how simplifying a biblical story might remove important elements. How could distillation enhance children's understanding of the same story?

5. Why is it important to anticipate the questions that children might ask about faith and theology?

Chapter 6

Orthodoxy and Theological Charity

I (Sam) remember my first trip to Los Angeles. I was in college and very excited to be in a really big city for the first time in my life. That trip turned out to be two of the most difficult weeks of my life. It started with a car accident and then a long wait for the repair in hotels that were far more affordable than they were safe. My mom was understandably worried about me. All my friends had left to go back to work and school, so I was there on my own. She called and had a friend of hers pick me up. Because I was staying in an area that was not really safe, my mom's friend had to wait for her husband to get off work to pick me up.

In this time before smartphones existed, while I was waiting for several hours, contemplating the meaning of life and looking out the window, I witnessed another accident. One car didn't see the other, and they hit each other. Neither was moving that fast, so the damage was minimal. The driver of the car that got hit got out, presumably to exchange information, but the other car backed up and started to leave. The driver who got hit started to yell at the other car as it drove away. The other car slowed down and turned around. At first, I was glad the driver who had caused the accident had decided to do the right thing. Then, to my surprise, instead of slowing down, he accelerated and tried to run over the other driver, who dove to safety as his car was struck a second time. I said out loud to myself, "I need to get out of here."

This is an appropriate analogy for our current political, spiritual, and relational climate. Things are bad out there, and then, just when we think people are starting to turn around, they hit the gas and try to run us over. If you have been in a theological debate on Twitter or Facebook, it happens fast—small disagreements will lead to you diving for safety almost out of nowhere. It seems like our culture has lost its ability to agree to disagree—to disagree and be friends.

THE PROBLEM: LACK OF CHARITY

In a recent article in *The Washington Examiner*, the author stated that "Among college-age people, 71% of Democrats said they would not go on a date with someone who voted for an opposing presidential candidate, the Generation Lab/*Axios* survey found."[1]

The church is no better in terms of disagreement; according to a recent Lifeway Research survey, "a majority (66%) of Americans ages 23–30 said they stopped attending church on a regular basis for at least a year after turning 18. Among their top reasons was that church members seemed divisive, judgmental, or hypocritical."[2]

Such data, telling us that when kids turn eighteen they leave the churches they grew up in, are far more common than we wish they were. Yet our experience tells us they are accurate. The division in our world is not limited to the world; it has come to the church. The challenge for us as followers of Christ is this: How do we teach and model to our kids a life that is marked by truth, grace, humility, conviction, and love?

You may be asking why there is a chapter on theological charity in a book on teaching theology to kids. It is because, for us as leaders, theology, when divorced from the person and work of Christ puffs us up and fills our hearts with the idea that we are right and all others are wrong. In 1 Corinthians 8:1 Paul says it this way: "Now concerning food offered to idols: we know that 'all of us possess knowledge.' This 'knowledge' puffs up, but love builds up." Charity humbles us to speak truth liberally and love extravagantly. The greatest opportunity we have as the church going forward to transform the real and perceived ways in which we are divisive, judgmental, and hypocritical is by extolling charity and demonstrating it to the kids we serve. It's by teaching our kids that God's love for us empowers us to love him and love others as a result.

We live in a world of black and white, of red states and blue states, and of theological infighting. We have all lost friends and, in some cases, family over politics, masks, and theological distinctions. We have an abundance of opinions. We lack truth, conviction, and love.

In our tribalistic culture, it can be easy to turn our opinions into dogma and turn molehills into mountains. In this chapter, we will explain the difference between orthodoxy (what Christians must believe) and secondary issues within the Christian faith, showing how to contend for the former while showing charity with the latter. Learning this distinction early on will not only help children humbly engage other points of view within orthodox Christianity but it will also sharpen their theological wisdom as they learn to discern between various perspectives and develop their own doctrinal convictions.

What we love and how we love will transform how we learn and how we disciple the next generation. James K. A. Smith poses this provocative question:

> What if you are defined not by what you know but by what you *desire*? What if the center and seat of the human person is found not in the heady regions of the intellect but in the gut-level regions of the heart? How would that change our approach to discipleship and Christian formation?[3]

What we think about informs what we love, and what we love informs how we love others. The right doctrine that we believe should inform the right practice that we do. Knowing is not enough; knowledge must transform our hearts and our actions so that our actions properly reflect who we love.

In this chapter, we have chosen to use the word *charity* even though it has fallen out of use and has been replaced in our time with the word *love*. To be clear, doing so isn't inaccurate. I prefer *charity* to *love* (where applicable) because it is more specifically understood. In our culture we have overused and misused the word *love*, and it has lost its meaning. We say, "I love coffee," "I love my friends," "I love my kids," and "I love God." All of those would be different words in Greek (the original language in which the New Testament was written).

Secondly, we have reduced love to an emotion we feel rather than actions we take because of emotions we feel. *Charity* is a word that can and does mean *love* yet has an active element to it. Charity is love received and love expressed. Kyle Borg sums it up this way: "Love's source is God Himself, and in showing us love He gives us a capacity to express charity—returning that love to Him and others."[4] God models love to us so that our love might be actively demonstrated to those around us. Charity is love in action.

What those kids in the Lifeway research failed to see was both a church that held steadfastly to deep biblical truths and a church that was so transformed by the love of God that they returned that love back to God and others. Charity is a receiving and giving love. What the church needs now more than ever is a recovery of biblical charity.

The Principle: Charity Is Essential for Good Theology

The apostle Paul penned these powerful words in his letter to the Corinthian church, words we would do well to ponder today:

> Though I speak with the tongues of men and of angels, and have not charity, I am become as sounding brass, or a tinkling cymbal. And though I have the gift of prophecy, and understand all mysteries, and all knowledge; and though I have all faith, so that I could remove mountains, and have not charity, I am nothing. And though I bestow all my goods to feed the poor, and though I give my body to be burned, and have not charity, it profiteth me nothing. (1 Corinthians 13:1–3 KJV)

Charity as a term and as a practice has fallen into disuse, but I believe the KJV helps us to understand what this virtue meant to Paul. For him, charity was not a feature of theology but was essential to it. What he is saying is that knowing all things isn't enough because the God we serve is Love (1 John 4:7–8). He is omniscient and knows all things, but his knowledge of all things is marked by a transcendent love.

Charity is the reason Christ came to save us

This idea of charity being a love that is giving and receiving love comes from the love that God has within himself. Michael Horton beautifully illustrates the love that God has for us and how he invites those who belong to him into the relationship he enjoys:

> Whenever God acts toward creatures, it is out of the complete relational satisfaction that he already enjoys as the Trinity. The eternally begotten Son lives from the love of the Father, but the Father is such because he has a Son, and in the Spirit, the Father and the Son not only have a third person to love but one who loves them in return and brings sinful creatures into the circle of that loving fellowship.[5]

It is out of the overflow of the love that God has within himself that, in an act of charity, he sent his Son to earth on behalf of human beings, in order to rescue and redeem those who were undeserving of that love. John 3:16 says, "For God so loved the world, that he gave his only Son, that whoever believes in him should not perish but have eternal life." This act of self-giving models to us the kind of love we, as image bearers (Genesis 1:26), are to walk in. This is *agape* love—charity.

Charity is the mode of Christ's ministry

Not only was the coming of Christ an act of charity but it was also the mode by which he ministered while he was here among us. John 1:14 says, "And the Word became flesh and dwelt among us, and we have seen his glory, glory as of the only Son from the Father, full of grace and truth." Jesus came not only as a gift but also as a revelation of what God is like.

The glory of God was on display in Jesus, who was full of grace and full of truth. He himself was truth incarnate, marked by a love that he received, a love that John was showing us in the mention of the Father and the Son. This was the mark of Jesus's ministry; he was truth (and full of truth) but was at the same time full of grace. This is what our lives should likewise reflect. Yet we often struggle because, in our right desire for truth, we forget Christ's own ministry to us. In doing this, "We make an idol of truth itself; for truth apart from charity is not God, but His image and idol, which we must neither love nor worship."[6] When we are full of truth but not full of charity, we distort the image of God we were created to reflect.

Charity is the message of Christ's death

Luke 23:34 tells us, "And Jesus said, 'Father, forgive them, for they know not what they do.'" On the cross the message of Jesus was one of forgiveness of sins. He took our place and died the death we, because of our sin, deserved to die. Jesus was forgiving not only those who had killed him but also all of us who put him there. Jesus starts by using the relational name of God, "Father," based on the nature of the love he has received and participates in, followed by giving us love in this act of forgiveness.

G. K. Chesterton believed that the cross is the greatest message and demonstration of charity. He spoke often of this and its importance:

> It is true that there is a thing crudely called charity, which means charity to the deserving poor; but charity to the deserving is not charity at all, but justice. It is the undeserving who require it.[7]

Here Chesterton clarifies what Christ modeled: that charity is truly charity when it is given to the undeserving. Chesterton elsewhere says that "charity means pardoning what is unpardonable, or it is no virtue at all."[8] Charity, as modeled by Christ, is the goal of the life of every Christian.

THE CIRCLES OF ORTHODOXY

Christian theological orthodoxy refers to the body of established and widely accepted beliefs and doctrines within the Christian faith. It represents the core tenets that have been recognized and affirmed by most Christian denominations and scholars throughout history.

There are certain things you must believe to be a Christian. There are other things you are free to disagree on and still be a Christian. My personal relationship with Jesus isn't what unites me to an African pastor on the other side of the world. What unites us is the truth we both hold that God Almighty is our Father (Genesis 17:1; Ephesians 4:6) that Jesus is the Word made flesh and the Son of God (John 1:14;

John 3:16), that Jesus was conceived by the Holy Spirit and born of a virgin (Matthew 1:20; Luke 1:35), lived a sinless life (Hebrews 4:15), and suffered (Mark 8:31) under Pontius Pilate (John 19:6)—who was a real person—that Jesus was crucified on a Roman cross (Mark 15:25; 1 Corinthians 15:3) and rose again (Luke 24:1–8; 1 Corinthians 15:4). We must believe in the Holy Spirit (John 14:26), one church and one unified body of believers (1 Corinthians 12:12–26; Hebrews 11), one baptism and the forgiveness of sin (Ephesians 4:5; Acts 2:38), and life everlasting (Mark 10:29–30).

Gavin Ortlund in his book *Finding the Right Hills to Die On* gives us four excellent questions to help us discern if a doctrine we are discussing is of primary importance:

1. How clear is the Bible on this doctrine?
2. What is the doctrine's importance to the gospel?
3. What is the testimony of the historical church concerning this doctrine?
4. What is the doctrine's effect upon the church today?[9]

While there are many more questions that could be asked, these questions are a mix of biblical, theological, historical, and practical questions that help form a grid by which we can help differentiate between doctrines that are primary and those that are secondary.

These central aspects of Christian orthodoxy include belief in the Holy Trinity, in the divinity of Jesus Christ, in salvation through him, and in the historic reality of his life, death, and resurrection. While variations exist among different Christian traditions, theological orthodoxy serves as a unifying framework that defines the fundamental beliefs and practices shared by most Christian communities, helping to distinguish them from heterodox or heretical views.

One way to think about what we must believe as Christians and what we are free to differ on is to think of orthodoxy as a set of circles. There are central truths that everyone must agree on to be Christian. Some examples are provided in Figure 4 below. If you deny the tenets of the Nicene Creed, you are something other than a Christian. But having a central standard of truth allows you to discern the difference between right and almost right. Knowing this, you should grow in your ability to be full of truth without separating it from charity as Pascal warned.

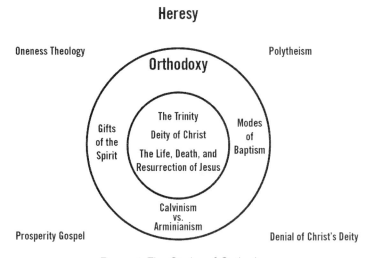

Figure 4. The Circles of Orthodoxy

Having a set of core doctrines that you agree on with other believers allows you to have much-needed common ground in which to discuss areas of disagreement. Take baptism, for example. As a Christian, you must believe that baptism is of significant importance but not saving importance because of the final command of Jesus (Matthew 28:19) and because it was modeled by Jesus (Matthew 3:15). That we should baptize is common ground on which we must agree. The mode of baptism is ground for charitable disagreement because the mode of baptism isn't specified in Scripture. Do we immerse completely or sprinkle? Do we baptize babies or only adults? Those concerns fall within the circles of orthodoxy. They are beyond the core of orthodoxy but are not against the teaching of Scripture and, therefore, not heresy. Because we have a common fundamental understanding about baptism, we can disagree well and be charitable in our interactions.

Having a fundamental understanding of biblical truth also allows us to identify when, in this case, baptism falls outside the circles of orthodoxy—when churches baptize people in only the name of Jesus and when they teach that baptism, not the person and work of Christ, saves you.

When you don't value Scripture and the faith handed to us (core doctrines and creeds) as primary, that lack of value is clearly seen in your actions and attitudes. When you understand the love that God has for you (and as a result you have for God), it is made manifest in how you treat others who are like you and especially those who differ from you (1 John 4:20). The result of not being driven by love is a tendency to become puffed up by your theological knowledge and to become subject to theological fads and personal hobbyhorses. The result of that tendency is a vigorous defense of secondary things because you have abandoned what is primary: "'You shall love the Lord your God with all your heart and with all your soul and with all your mind and with all your strength.' The second is this: 'You shall love your neighbor as yourself.'" (Mark 12:30–31). This is why so much of the internet is filled with uncharitable conversations. We do the social media equivalent of turning our car around and trying to run down our fellow drivers.

Clarity is itself an act of charity. We live in a world in which the culture and, even in some cases, churches are espousing the belief that you can be what you want to be and do what you want to do. Charity is informed by the truth of who God is and defined by his love toward us in Christ.

When we see that truth and love in Scripture and in our communities, we are, as a result, more charitable in our interactions with others. When I realize how much I have been loved and forgiven, I am more willing to love and forgive others as part of my interactions with them.

If you know someone who differs on something inside the circle of orthodoxy, engage, but make sure your comments are seasoned with charity. When engaging those who are outside of the circle of orthodoxy, do not back down from what is true, but do so with love. Jesus was the perfect man. He came to earth as John says, "And the Word became flesh and dwelt among us, and we have seen his glory, glory as of the only Son from the Father, full of grace and truth" (John 1:14). He was full of grace and truth, and we are to imitate him and those who are imitating him (1 Corinthians 11:1).

In Acts 18:24–26 NIV we see this type of charitable interaction take place. Two prominent leaders in the church, Priscilla and Aquila, listened to the gifted oration of Apollos, but saw that he needed further instruction:

> Meanwhile a Jew named Apollos, a native of Alexandria, came to Ephesus. He was a learned man, with a thorough knowledge of the Scriptures. He had been instructed in the way of the Lord, and he spoke with great fervor and taught about Jesus accurately, though he knew only the baptism of John. He began to speak boldly in the synagogue. When Priscilla and Aquila heard him, they invited him to their home and explained to him the way of God more adequately.

What we see here is an example of the virtue of charity on both ends of the conversation. We see the humility of Priscilla and Aquila to hear Apollos out and then to speak with him personally and directly about the accuracy of his well-delivered teaching. They taught him about the way of God more accurately. They lovingly explained about Jesus and baptism in his name. The understanding of what baptism is for is central to Christian teaching. How Priscilla and Aquila handled Apollos's understanding in person and how Apollos received their instruction together form a great example of charity. We must boldly correct our brothers and sisters in love. We likewise need to receive correction in an attitude of grace and charity.

We must not ignore fundamental orthodox truths because culture and psychology tell us they are unpopular. We must distill truth with charity and winsomeness. Nonetheless, we must speak the truth, but that truth must be seasoned by love.

THE RULE OF LOVE

The root of every sin is a lack of charity. Augustine, in the fourth century, said that love (or charity) should be the central aspect of every Christian because John says clearly and without equivocation that God is love. In fact, John says, in 1 John 4:8, that if you do not love, you don't know God because God is love. Augustine further explains the many different aspects of loving rightly:

> Now he is a man of just and holy life who forms an unprejudiced estimate of things, and keeps his affections also under strict control, so that he neither loves what he ought not to love, nor fails to love what he ought to love, nor loves that more which ought to be loved less, nor loves that equally which ought to be loved either less or more, nor loves that less or more which ought to be loved equally. No sinner is to be loved as a sinner; and every man is to be loved as a man for God's sake; but God is to be loved for His own sake. And if God is to be loved more than any man, each man ought to love God more than himself.[10]

In the fourteenth century, Dante picked up and expanded on this idea of love. Charity was the central point of *The Divine Comedy* and the highest goal of a Christian. In the very middle of his massive epic, Dante says that our lives are to be lived in love and marked by love. He says that every virtue is cultivated in love, and every vice is found in the result of broken love. Deficient love is the failure to appropriately love who or what we should. Misdirected love is the love of the wrong things, which results in envy, wrath, and pride, and excessive love is marked by gluttony and lust. Fundamentally, Dante is saying that the root of all our faults and failures is a lack of charity—a broken love.

Love is central to the life of every believer. Paul says at the end of 1 Corinthians that we are all uniquely gifted. None of us are exactly the same. We have been given gifts for the good of the church and the glory of God. He then says the motivation and the use of our gifts must be the same: love, rather than fame or personal glory. The foundation of our service to God and others must be charity.

In 1 Corinthians 13:1–3 Paul says,

> If I speak in the tongues of men and of angels, but have not love, I am a noisy gong or a clanging cymbal. And if I have prophetic powers, and understand all mysteries and all knowledge, and if I have all faith, so as to remove mountains, but have not love, I am nothing. If I give away all I have, and if I deliver up my body to be burned, but have not love, I gain nothing.

Don't skim over this familiar passage. Let its weight sink in: "If I give my body to be burned, but have not love, I gain NOTHING."

Lest we think that the supremacy of love is Paul's idea, consider Jesus's response in Mark 12:28–31 when he was asked to identify the greatest commandment:

And one of the scribes came up and heard them disputing with one another, and seeing that he answered them well, asked him, "Which commandment is the most important of all?" Jesus answered, "The most important is, 'Hear, O Israel: The Lord our God, the Lord is one. And you shall love the Lord your God with all your heart and with all your soul and with all your mind and with all your strength.' The second is this: 'You shall love your neighbor as yourself.' There is no other commandment greater than these."

The greatest commandment is to love God, and obedience to this command will be seen in our supernatural charity toward others. By the power of the Holy Spirit, we love others more than we naturally love ourselves.

If external, historical, and biblical truth is our standard, if charity is our mode, and if love is our goal, we will be able to teach our kids not only what is true but also how to live that truth in a life marked by love for God— love which is seen by others in our love for people.

I pray this section has helped you reflect upon the ways you understand and teach the value of charity to the kids you lead. Our kids can grow up and do many amazing things. They could give all their goods to feed the poor, they could give their bodies to be burned, but if they do not have charity, it profits them nothing. That is a strong statement coming from a man who wrote more theology than we will learn and who was put to death for proclaiming those truths. If he did not have charity, those things profited him nothing.

I think a fitting way to close this section is with a reminder from Paul Wadell that charity is not an accessory to the Christian life but the center and the summit of it:

Charity is both the center and summit of the Christian life because through friendship with God human beings increasingly participate in their greatest possible good. Such intimate communion with God leads to an abiding and ever-growing love for one's neighbors.[11]

Take a moment to put this book down and ask God to help you be more aware of the ways you have lacked the kind of charity that should be central and ever-increasing in your walk with Christ.

THE PRACTICE: WALK IN LOVE

As I have said before, the word *love*, in a culture that is obsessed with love, has lost its meaning to such an extent that I think using other words for it, when appropriate, is a good idea. We need to reclaim charity and the fruit of charity in our lives. We must be as equally passionate about orthodoxy (right belief) as we are about orthopraxy (right action). Our kids must see us model both in our lives, including in how we live in front of them and how we express ourselves when we don't even realize they are watching us, because kids notice every interaction and pick up on subtleties more than we realize. We must proactively teach them the principles of charity and model what charity looks like in the life of a person transformed by the gospel. Our interactions with other Christians and non-Christians alike should be marked by charity.

Teach the importance of mercy as a form of love

Emphasize to children that love is the central value in both their interactions with others and their faith. We should connect every story we teach to the radical nature of God's mercy on us, through which he expressed his love for us. Seeing the Scriptures in light of this is a great way to instill within kids an ability to see the redemptive love of God on display in every Bible story we tell. God shows mercy to us because he loves us. Why does he love us? Because he loves us. Further, God expects us to love other people, and to demonstrate that love by showing mercy. One of the great stories that teaches the importance of loving our neighbor is the parable of the good Samaritan. In this parable, Jesus drives us to a place where we have to look somewhere for our motivation. We are left with two options: One is temporal; the other is eternal. One is sufficient; the other is completely insufficient. We can either show mercy because we are supposed to show mercy, or we can show mercy because we genuinely care about other people.

Where Jesus takes this lawyer is where he takes you and me. He puts a priest and a Levite in the story—both of whom had the job of taking care of the poor. When it came to personal involvement and sacrifice, they saw the need, they decided the cost was too great, and they went to the other side of the road. They refused to show mercy. A "do what you're supposed to" morality can only get you so far. It will always leave you unchanged and those around you unimpressed.

In my life, my motivation changed when I realized that moral goodness—doing what I was supposed to—alone could not save me. This story of the good Samaritan is a perfect example. I read this story and have told this story more times than I can remember. I always read that and told others that the motivation of this parable was to love your enemies. That is certainly a truth you can draw from this text, but the great truth that Jesus was driving to the young lawyer was found in who was in need. If this parable were about loving your enemy, the person who was beaten up would have been a Samaritan. That, in itself, would have been shocking enough. Jesus brings it to a whole other level. The hero of the story was a Samaritan, and it's in our hero that we find our motivation to properly love and show mercy to our enemies.

The story of the good Samaritan is not primarily about us loving our enemies. It's about how our enemy loved us.

We are not the good Samaritan in the story. We are the man who got beaten up by robbers. Jesus is the good Samaritan. This is the basis for us living a life of love. We love because we have been loved. Jesus proved his love through his sacrifice for us.

Not only is that the case, but also our union with Christ, which comes as a result of faith in him, empowers us to love and show mercy to others. Jesus said in John 15:4–5,

> "Abide in me, and I in you. As the branch cannot bear fruit by itself, unless it abides in the vine, neither can you, unless you abide in me. I am the vine; you are the branches. Whoever abides in me and I in him, he it is that bears much fruit, for apart from me you can do nothing."

This practice is what gives us the ability to love as Christ commands. If the root is good (abiding in Christ) the fruit will naturally follow (love for others).

Explain the difference between core beliefs and secondary issues

Help children understand that there are essential core beliefs in their faith, such as the belief in the Holy Trinity and the divinity of Jesus, that are nonnegotiable. Teach them that it's OK to have differing opinions on secondary issues like spiritual gifts or other non-core beliefs. Core issues are clearly taught in Scripture and are generally around the person and work of Christ, the necessity of the ordinances, issues pertaining to salvation, the authority of Scripture, and the gospel. Secondary issues, although important, are things that have to do with preference and are usually unclear from Scripture. Another consideration can be summarized by these questions: What has the church historically believed about this doctrine? What is the result of believing and acting on this doctrine in my life and the life of my church?

When talking about essentials like the Trinity, be sure to tell them that these essentials are what all Christians must believe. At other times, you may be talking about baptism or the gifts of the Spirit, explaining that these beliefs are important, but many Christians differ on what they believe about these ideas.

Teach that love should be present in all our interactions

Teach children that love should be at the center of their interactions with others. Whether they're discussing theological matters or dealing with everyday conflicts, they should strive to be kind and charitable, even when they disagree.

We live in a world that prioritizes tolerance and tells our kids that love is love. As Christians, we know God is love. The center of every interaction and the goal of every communication should be grounded in love. Paul tells us that our love for others is based on a love that we have received from God. This love is not defined by how we feel or what we think is true. It's based on a person and his love for us. It's based on a set of external truths that guide us in every interaction. Colossians 3:11–13 provides a beautiful picture of what love looks like in action:

> Here there is not Greek and Jew, circumcised and uncircumcised, barbarian, Scythian, slave, free; but Christ is all, and in all. Put on then, as God's chosen ones, holy and beloved, compassionate hearts, kindness, humility, meekness, and patience, bearing with one another and, if one has a complaint against another, forgiving each other; as the Lord has forgiven you, so you also must forgive.

Model charitable behavior

Lead by example. Demonstrate how to engage in charitable discussions and how to disagree respectfully. Show children that it's possible to maintain strong convictions while treating others with love and respect. It might be helpful to select a particular issue (especially with older children) and give them a basic introduction to both sides of that issue. Make sure to include passages of Scripture that support both or all positions on the issue. Be fair in the way that you represent every side—don't misrepresent one position's arguments to make it easier to disprove, especially if it's the position with which you personally disagree. Also, be accurate in describing the position—use the best scholars on all sides of the issue as your sources.

In your interactions with kids, model the behavior you want them to practice. This is important for kids who have behavior issues. Holding them to expectations (truth), yet communicating those with clarity and love, makes all the difference in the world. Show up when kids are going through difficulty like parents divorcing or when they are going to the hospital for surgery. There are many ways to model charity to the kids we lead. Most of the time it doesn't cost a ton of money; it just requires you showing up and pointing them to Jesus.

> Kids hear what you teach them, but they remember who you are much longer than what you say.

We, as Christians, are called to put on love. Colossians 3 continues in verses 14–15 by saying, "And above all these put on love, which binds everything together in perfect harmony. And let the peace of Christ rule in your hearts, to which indeed you were called in one body. And be thankful."

Highlight the value of unity and common ground

Focus on the common values and beliefs that Christians share and how these can be a source of unity. Look for ways to teach kids the fundamentals of their faith and the importance of creeds. The Apostles' Creed, the Nicene Creed, and catechisms are excellent ways for kids to understand what we believe and to know both the common ground we have with other Christians and how that differs from other faiths, so memorizing these can be helpful.

Stress the importance of love as a commandment

Teach children that love is not just a suggestion but a commandment (Mark 12:28–31). Help them understand that showing love to God and others is a fundamental aspect of their faith. The command to love is a command to follow the example of Christ, who empowers our ability to love because he first loved us (1 John 4:19).

One of the greatest acts of charity we can do for kids is teach them how to apologize. We do this in two ways: the first is by asking them for forgiveness when we have sinned, and the second is by training them how to ask for forgiveness. We also need to make sure that kids know that they do not only need to ask for forgiveness when they have done something wrong. They also need to ask for forgiveness when they recognize that they have not done something right and then they need to correct their behavior. When kids are forced to apologize, they will often say a halfhearted "sorry." When teaching kids to ask for forgiveness, you have them do three things:

1. Say "I'm sorry for _____" and have them name their deed specifically: "I am sorry I lied, stole money, made fun of you," or whatever the sin may be.
2. Then have them say, "Would you please forgive me?"
3. Finally, have them say, "I will ask God for help to not do it again."

In apologizing to kids and training them to do the same, you are teaching them to be more charitable because they see that when you are not charitable, there are consequences, and you will need to own the ways you have sinned against someone else.

Foster respect and compassion for others

Encourage children to put themselves in others' shoes and consider how their words and actions affect others. Help them recognize the feelings and perspectives of those they interact with. We should treat others how we want to be treated (Matthew 7:12). This rule is helpful for kids who may not have confessed their need for God's help with a particular situation or who may not have admitted their need for redemption through Christ. Those who have placed their trust in God's mercy need to be reminded to treat others not just how we want to be treated but to treat them the way God in Christ has treated us. (At the same time, we need to recognize that treating others with love does not necessarily mean that we avoid hurting their feelings. Christ gives us our ultimate example of love, but, as John says, Jesus was "full of grace and truth" [John 1:14]).

We were once strangers, but in Jesus we have been brought near to God. As Paul declares in Ephesians 2:12–13,

> Remember that you were at that time separated from Christ, alienated from the commonwealth of Israel and strangers to the covenants of promise, having no hope and without God in the world. But now in Christ Jesus you who once were far off have been brought near by the blood of Christ.

We should have been treated as strangers and enemies, but because of Jesus we are now friends.

We can also foster compassion for others by teaching your kids about other cultures and beliefs, explaining the importance of missions, and telling the stories of famous missionaries are great ways to foster charity in their interactions with people from different cultures. Teaching our kids that we are made in the image of God (Genesis 1:27) is essential. We all look different and see the world through different eyes, but it is in the multifaceted cultures we represent that we reflect the beauty of a multi-dimensional God.

One final suggestion would be to help develop a connection with the church around the world by having special guests come into your services and share about what God is doing in the church around the world. The most important things, however, are helping your kids understand the need for the gospel in every country and teaching your kids to pray for the church they attend and the church around the world.

Create opportunities for acts of love

Involve children in charitable activities, such as volunteering, helping those in need, or participating in church or community service projects. These experiences can reinforce the importance of charity and love.

It doesn't even have to be as elaborate as a community project. Teach kids to serve each other by serving snacks, handing out craft supplies, and cleaning up after a small group is done. Small acts of service train our kids to serve others as they have been served by others.

Giving kids an opportunity to act on what they have learned in class or kids' church is a great exercise in applying truth. Knowledge puffs up when it is not applied. If knowledge of God becomes an accumulation of unused facts, rather than a collection of truths that guide our lives and direct our loves, we will be filled with pride rather than poured out in love.

This is also a challenge for us as leaders to not just teach abstract truths but also to make those truths practical and to find ways for parents and kids to practice what we have taught them and what they have learned.

When we talk about stories from the Bible like the parable of the good Samaritan, we as teachers need to ask, "What are ways we can show the mercy and love of God to our enemies like God has shown mercy and love to us?"

Having a robust theology is essential, particularly in the present age. But if we don't have love, our knowledge of God is worthless.

DISCUSSION QUESTIONS

1. What does the author mean by "theological charity," and why is it important, especially in the context of teaching kids theology?

2. According to the author, what is the difference between orthodoxy (core Christian beliefs) and secondary issues in the Christian faith? Why is understanding this difference crucial?

3. What analogy does the author use to describe Christian theological orthodoxy? How does having a shared core of beliefs benefit Christians in their interactions and discussions with one another?

4. Why does the author suggest memorizing creeds like the Apostles' Creed and Nicene Creed? How can these creeds help Christians understand common ground and differences in faith?

5. How can parents and teachers practically teach children the principles and practice of charity? Consider the examples and activities mentioned in the chapter and try to think of some of your own.

Chapter 7

Pathways: Developing a Plan for Teaching Kids Theology

One summer in high school, I (Hunter) went hiking with some friends to a popular spot in our town called "The Blue Hole." As you can probably guess from the name, this is a swimming hole surrounded by large rocks, tall trees, and jagged cliffs, making it a perfect place to cool off in the humid hills of Tennessee.

There's a well-worn path that generations of locals have trekked to get to this oasis, but I wanted to chart my own course. Most of the group wanted to stick to the tried-and-true trail, but one of my friends agreed to take the road less traveled (or never traveled, in this case).

So off we went. My friend and I waded through the uncharted brush, climbed hills, and crossed rivers. Eventually, after taking a few breaks and getting lost, we reached our destination. The rest of the group had been swimming for quite some time and were ready to leave when we arrived. I was disappointed. Cutting through the woods like a world explorer was fun, but missing out on the Blue Hole with my friends made the excursion pointless. What good was the journey without the destination? Trading the tried-and-true for the unique and new wasn't all it was cracked up to be. My obsession with doing something different meant that I forfeited my opportunity to do what mattered.

THE PROBLEM: WRONG CRITERIA FOR CHOOSING PATHWAYS

If you've served in children's ministry for any length of time, you've probably noticed the never-ending cycle of curricula, resources, and products released for churches. Along with these new releases, most kids' ministry conferences trade on the promise of attendees receiving fresh ideas, tools, and methods for their ministries. While there's nothing wrong with adopting new curricula and methodologies, the obsession with what's new or "hot" in children's ministry can overshadow more fundamental questions. Choosing a pathway because "it's never been done before" is just as bad as (or worse than) sticking with something because "it's always been done." Both reasons use the wrong metric to measure the fruitfulness of a method.

To choose the best methods or "pathways" for teaching kids theology, you must first establish criteria for evaluating a potential pathway's truthfulness, goodness, and beauty. You need a firm understanding of your ministry's vision, mission, and philosophy to do this.

Vision : The destination (your "why")

You've probably heard of churches or businesses having a vision statement. Without a vision or desired goal, an organization has no direction. Your ministry's vision serves as the destination toward which every leader, teacher, and volunteer strives. It's the "why" behind everything you do! Without a clearly defined destination, people will waste valuable time and resources pursuing vague aspirations and ideals.

Ask yourself, "Does our children's ministry have a clearly defined goal, purpose, or destination?" If not, it needs to become top priority.

> Without knowing where you're going, you can't assess if your path is taking your kids in the right direction. The North Star of your vision keeps you from taking every path that comes your way and helps you choose the ones that best serve your kids.

To create or evaluate your vision statement, take the time to ask yourself these questions:

- What has God called us to do in our church and community?
- What is the scope of our ministry and the outcome we desire to see?
- What do we want our kids to become?
- What need does our ministry fulfill?

Every children's ministry is called to proclaim the gospel and disciple its kids (Matthew 28:19–20), but composing a vision statement that articulates the Great Commission with your church's specific language and context in mind provides greater clarity to what your ministry is seeking to accomplish.

Mission : The vehicle (your "what")

Your vision serves as the destination of your ministry, and your mission serves as the vehicle that gets you there. It's the "what" of your ministry. This is why your vision must be established first. Knowing where you're going helps you determine the best vehicle for the journey.

For example, if you're going to a store down the street, you may only need good tennis shoes for walking or a bike for riding. If you're going to a friend's house an hour away, you'll probably choose to drive your car, or if you're planning to attend an event on the other side of the country, you'll most likely book a flight. Likewise, your vision (the destination) determines your mission (the vehicle you'll use) to get there.

Awana (a nonprofit organization that reaches millions of kids worldwide) is a great example of a ministry whose mission serves its vision. Awana's vision is that "all children and youth around the world will come to know, love, and serve the Lord Jesus Christ." Its mission is to "equip leaders to reach kids with the gospel and engage them in lifelong discipleship."[1] Since Awana's vision is global in scope and specific in outcome, it needs a vehicle that balances both well, which is why its mission is to equip leaders. Equipping local leaders to reach and disciple kids in their context better positions Awana to help children and youth around the world know, love, and serve Jesus Christ.

As you consider your mission, prayerfully ask the following questions:

- What are the best actions that lead to our destination?
- Is there anything we are doing that hinders us from accomplishing our vision?
- Do we need to adapt what we are doing to better fulfill our ministry's purpose?

To answer these questions effectively, you need to understand the final piece, which is your ministry's philosophy.

Philosophy: The parameters (your "how")

If your mission is the vehicle that gets you to your destination, then your ministry's philosophy serves as the parameters that help you determine your vehicle's best use and route. Philosophy isn't discussed as often as vision or mission, but it's just as important. Your philosophy is made up of the deep-rooted values that influence the decision-making of your ministry. It's the "how" behind your "what." Without a well-pondered philosophy, you might take unnecessary detours or underutilize the vehicles in your ministry.

For example, you can have "making faithful disciples" as your vision with "teaching robust theology" as part of your mission, but your philosophy (the deep-rooted values of your ministry) will set the parameters for how you decide to teach theology to your kids.

For instance, if a ministry strongly values study and knowledge, they might opt for a content-heavy teaching method. Or, if a ministry values fun and excellence, they might heavily rely on videos or elaborate object lessons. A ministry might place great value on relationships and choose a low-tech approach, emphasizing small-group engagement. Some might focus on biblical literacy and elevate the use of Bible skills and memorization, while others emphasize service and teaching through activities and experiences. Do you see why pondering and articulating your ministry's philosophy is so important? Your values radically alter your practices. It's why two churches can have similar visions and use the same resources yet operate differently. Just as the parameters set on a GPS dictate the specific route it recommends (such as the shortest distance or the fastest time), your philosophy will dictate the methodology and resources your church will adopt.

To produce or assess your values, you can ask yourself these questions:

- What are our church's stated values, and how are they displayed in the practices of our ministry?
- What do our current practices reveal about what we truly value?
- Are there any values we're lacking that we should aspire to uphold?

Your church most likely has a vision or mission statements it already uses. It would be wise to have the children's ministry adopt as many of those statements as possible and adjust those statements where needed. If neither your church nor your children's ministry has a written vision, mission, or philosophy statement, you can use the guidelines provided in this chapter to start creating a mission, vision, or philosophy statement. Again, clearly defining the vision, vehicle, and values (or philosophy) of your ministry will provide you with the criteria needed to pick the best pathways for teaching kids theology in your ministry.

The Principle: Pathways Shape Theology

I once took a trip to Florida with my family. The beach was clean, the weather was nice, and the food was delicious. Everything about the destination was perfect, but if you were to ask my kids what they remember most from that trip, they would say one thing: the giant peanut. On the drive down, we went through Dothan, a small town in Alabama known as the "peanut capital of the world." The city is full of goofy peanut statues, but the one my kids recall is the thirty-foot-tall statue outside the grounds of the National Peanut Festival. This giant peanut is seared into their memories because I made a point to stop, get out of the van, and take pictures with it. This only took a minute or two, but the moment has affected my kids.

When it comes to the discipleship of our children, the destination is primary, but the journey is highly formative. Not only is *what* we're teaching our kids about God paramount but also *how* we decide to teach theology is also important. Our methods can shape our kids just as much as our message. Scripture speaks to the powerful link between our message and the methods we use to form our children.

Declaration and retention

When it comes to our message or content, we're called to declare nothing less to the next generation than the glory and goodness of God. In Psalm 78:1–4, the psalmist urges the people to hear his teaching and relay it to the coming generations:

> Give ear, O my people, to my teaching;
> > incline your ears to the words of my mouth!
> I will open my mouth in a parable;
> > I will utter dark sayings from of old,
> things that we have heard and known,
> > that our fathers have told us.
> We will not hide them from their children,
> > but tell to the coming generation
> the glorious deeds of the LORD and his might,
> > and the wonders that he has done.

Notice the teaching isn't a new revelation but "of old." It is made up of things that were "heard and known." The older generation isn't called to produce a new message of relevance or transfer moralistic platitudes. They are to declare God's glorious deeds, wonders, and might. David echoes this charge in Psalm 145: "Great is the LORD, and greatly to be praised, and his greatness is unsearchable. One generation shall commend your works to another, and shall declare your mighty acts" (vv. 3–4).

Again, we see the call for one generation to declare the mighty acts of God to the next. Scripture is clear that the pathways we choose must make much of God, praising him for who he is and what he has done. We must utilize methods that rely heavily on Scripture to do this effectively. We must choose pathways that rehearse its stories, echo its precepts, and stand on its promises.

Along with declaring God's glory and deeds, an interesting theme of remembrance is sprinkled throughout the Old Testament, particularly through memorial stones. After Israel miraculously crossed the Jordan River, God commanded

Joshua to set up twelve stones to memorialize the event. After Joshua relays God's commands and sets up the stones, he says:

> "When your children ask their fathers in times to come, 'What do these stones mean?' then you shall let your children know, 'Israel passed over this Jordan on dry ground.' For the LORD your God dried up the waters of the Jordan for you until you passed over, as the LORD your God did to the Red Sea, which he dried up for us until we passed over, so that all the peoples of the earth may know that the hand of the LORD is mighty, that you may fear the LORD your God forever." (Joshua 4:21b–24)

The stones served as a teaching mechanism to remind the adults and the children about the mighty works of God displayed at the Jordan. We see a similar teaching device used in 1 Samuel 7 when Samuel sets up a stone that he calls an "Ebenezer" ("stone of help") as a memorial to God's power in delivering Israel from the hands of the Philistines.

From these few passages, we see that declaration and retention go hand in hand. We are to declare what is true and do so in a memorable way. We are to proclaim God's glory, then set up "mental Ebenezers" that help our kids retain and live out the truth wherever they go.

Retention is key because if kids don't retain the truth we teach, they won't carry it outside our classrooms and churches. Kids can't live out what they don't remember. Of course, God's Word never returns void (Isaiah 55:11 KJV), but Scripture is clear that what we retain in us will remain with us wherever we go. Consider Psalm 119:11, which says, "I have stored up your word in my heart, that I might not sin against you." The psalmist didn't memorize God's Word purely for knowledge acquisition. He hid God's Word in his heart so that the words in him would flow out of him in moments of temptation. The psalmist understood the value of memorizing and meditating on God's Word (Psalm 119:15).

When God's Word isn't internalized, it becomes trivialized in the practical moments of life. Just look at the Israelites in the book of Judges. The older generations did not declare the works of God to their kids, and this failure resulted in their children not knowing who God was or what he had done (Judges 2:10). Even after seeing the miraculous deeds of God in the life of Gideon, Israel "did not remember the Lord their God" (Judges 8:34b). The best pathways declare the truth of God and help kids retain it by erecting stones of help in their minds—methods of remembering which aid them in recalling God's Word and applying it faithfully in times of need.

Entertainment and attention

If we're not careful, we can allow other criteria to shape our pathways for teaching kids. We can allow the influence of social media and the fast-paced nature of our culture to draw us away from declaration and retention and push us toward entertainment and keeping attention. "So what?" you might retort. "What's wrong with wanting to keep kids engaged? Are you saying we shouldn't make our methods fun or keep children's attention while we teach?" Not at all! There's nothing wrong with fun crafts, engaging activities, or captivating illustrations. Entertainment and keeping attention are phenomenal means for teaching theology, but they make horrible ends. If we make entertainment the goal, we can unintentionally make Scripture appear silly to our kids or twist its interpretation to fit our fun-driven objectives. Likewise, if we make keeping attention our primary goal, kids may stay engaged during our teaching time, but it doesn't mean they have comprehended or retained anything we've said. Keeping your kids' attention should be seen as a means to an end (the true goal, which is retention).[2]

What's the difference between using entertainment and attention as tools and upholding them as goals? I think a mission trip I took in high school can help reveal the difference.

I went on a mission trip to another state to serve inner-city kids and was put in charge of leading a small group of kids after the main teaching event. I wanted to ensure each day was packed with excitement, so I stacked several activities and songs on top of one another to avoid downtime in our schedule. My selections were not bad ideas in themselves, but my fixation with wanting the kids to have fun led me to choose activities and music that were disconnected from one another. They had nothing to do with the main themes or truths being communicated by our leaders. The kids had a blast, and I know they appreciated the care I had for them. However, my impact could have been greater if I had been more intentional with the songs and games I had chosen. It's true that I got their attention, but what would they remember? Yes, they had fun, but was the truth we presented clear? If I had seen fun and attention as tools, I would have chosen activities that reinforced the truths we were teaching and picked songs that would have made those same truths hard to forget.

Tried-and-true pathways

As we've seen, declaration and retention are God's prescribed means of forming children into his faithful followers, but what tools and methods best declare God's truth and help kids retain it? Thankfully, we don't have to reinvent the wheel. For centuries, the church has used methods of declaration and retention that have stood the test of time. They're like well-worn paths that have guided generations of teachers toward faithful discipleship. We would like to share some of those tried-and-true (yet sometimes forgotten) paths of generational discipleship.

Scripture memory

Scripture memory is a pathway that has been used to declare and retain the truth of God's Word since the Bible was first written. The Bible itself encourages this practice. Colossians 3:16a says, "Let the word of Christ dwell in you richly." In Deuteronomy 6:6–9, Moses tells the people that God's truth should be in their hearts, cherished, and spoken of in all places. This practice is commended for good reason. Scripture memory guards us against sin (Psalm 119:9–11), guides our hearts (Psalm 119:105), and helps us grow in holiness (Psalm 1:1–3). It fuels meditation and develops wisdom. Eugene Peterson has this to say about the power of Scripture memory.

> Memory is a databank we use to evaluate our position and make decisions. With a biblical memory, we have two thousand years of experience from which to make the off-the-cuff responses that are required each day in the life of faith. If we are going to live adequately and maturely as the people of God, we need more data to work from than our own experience can give us.[3]

When I lived in Chicago, I would evangelize on the city's streets and subways with some college friends. As I facilitated conversations and answered questions from skeptics, Bible verses would flood my mind. I would often quote Scripture that I had memorized as a kid. Certain words or phrases would trigger my memory (like a mental Ebenezer) and lead me to recall Bible passages I hadn't pondered in a long time.

If we want to make the most of this ancient practice, we must give it time and attention. It needs to be seen as significant and celebrated among our kids. Most curricula provide memory verses that go along with their lessons, and we would do well to capitalize on the resources they provide to make storing God's words easy and engaging. If your curriculum doesn't provide resources for Scripture memory, consider some of the resources and tips below:

- *Sing It* - Ministries such as Doorpost Songs, Seeds Kids Worship, and Songs for Saplings put Scripture to memorable, catchy tunes. Singing these songs is a great way to retain God's Word.
- *Act It* - Put hand motions to each word or phrase of a Bible passage you are memorizing. You can make up your own or find examples online.
- *Build It* - Write each word of a Bible passage on a block, cup, or Lego. Have kids work together to stack the items until the verse is in the right order. Making this a game not only makes Scripture memory fun, but it can also improve retention by tying memorization to an engaging experience.
- *Relay It* - Don't just review memory verses in your children's ministry. Invite parents to aid in the process. Relay the passage you are learning, and equip them to memorize it with their children. Parents can use apps like VerseLocker or songs from the ministries listed above to make Scripture memory engaging at home.

If we want our kids to think God's thoughts after him, committing his words to memory is a natural step in making it a reality.

Creeds

"Why do kids need to learn creeds? Shouldn't we just teach them the Bible?" These aren't uncommon questions. Creeds seem archaic and out of date, but the truth is that we live by creeds all the time. Even the phrase, "No creed but the Bible," is itself a creed. Creeds are simply statements of belief, and the early church creeds provided Christians with succinct, easy-to-remember summaries of doctrine. Creeds not only help us know what we believe but they also help us guard against falsehood. The ecumenical creeds were written to fight against heresies that denied core doctrines. Having kids learn these timeless creeds can help them know what they believe and defend against the lies of secular culture and religious beliefs outside the bounds of orthodoxy.

One of the most ancient and accessible creeds to teach children is the Apostles' Creed. It is one of the earliest summaries of the Christian faith. This creed could be reviewed before lessons or times of singing. It can also be used as a template for teaching kids the core doctrines of the Christian faith. Here are two resources to familiarize yourself with creeds and make you more comfortable with declaring their teachings:

- Apostles' Creed Cards - This set of cards from *Tiny Theologians* works line-by-line through the Apostles' Creed. The fun colors and inviting design help kids learn why the creed was originally written.
- *Know the Creeds and Councils* by Justin Holcomb - Holcomb's explanation of the ancient creeds and councils in their historical contexts will give you a greater appreciation for what Christians believe and will show you how these statements of faith have ongoing relevance for us in today's world.

Catechisms

"Catechism" or "catechize" aren't words we use every day, but they describe a process kids are engaged in consistently. "The terms related to catechesis," as Joe Carter

describes, "are derived from the original Greek word trans-
literated as *katecheo* (i.e., to teach orally, to instruct)."[4] In
short, to "catechize" means to teach. Historically, the church
has taught or "catechized" children through a question-and-
answer format. Whether you use the *Heidelberg Catechism*,
the *Westminster Shorter Catechism*, or another catechism, you
will see questions posed on certain points of doctrine and
answers provided to be memorized and discussed.

Initially, this method might seem dull. Having kids
memorize answers to questions may not sound thrilling or
fun, but don't knock it until you've tried it. There are several reasons why this method has been used for centuries
and continues to bear fruit today. For one, it capitalizes on
the memorizing power of children. Memorization reaches
its peak quality and extent during childhood and is usually unmatched at any other stage of a person's life. Second,
catechisms are designed to be cross-congregational, meaning that the questions kids answer and memorize can also
be learned by adults. Third, since kids and adults can use
this tool in discipleship, it creates a dialogue and community among the members of the church around the truths
of the gospel. Tim Keller says, "Catechesis is different from
listening to a sermon or lecture—or reading a book—in that
it is deeply communal and participatory. The practice of
question-answer recitation brings instructors and students
into a naturally interactive, dialogical process of learning."[5]
The dialogical nature of this method cultivates relationships
and develops ownership of the truths being learned. Fourth,
the writers of these catechisms put a great deal of thought,
prayer, and study into their questions and aimed to consider
the whole counsel of God in how they answered them. I can't
tell you how many times we have used the faithful language
of these catechisms to answer our kids' questions about God.
Last, catechisms teach children to expect questions about

their faith. As they grow older, our kids will be questioned by their friends, classmates, and coworkers on the content of and reasons for their faith. Catechisms prepare our kids for such moments by helping them know what they believe and why.

Since catechisms have been used for centuries and continue to be made today, knowing where to start can be overwhelming. While each is unique, most cover similar topics, such as the nature of God, the Apostles' Creed, the Lord's Prayer, and the Ten Commandments. Some have questions and answers that fit better within certain denominations and traditions, so we encourage you to research a catechism's history and theological framework before committing to it. Below are some helpful resources to get you started.

- Modern Catechisms
  - *New City Catechism* – This catechism teaches core doctrines of the Christian faith through fifty-two questions and answers and offers a variety of supplementary resources such as devotionals, curriculum, and a well-designed app.[6]
  - *Cross Formed Kids* – This original catechism aims to teach kids everything they need to know to read and understand Scripture for a lifetime. It has 108 questions that come with coaching videos, lessons, activities, and well-produced songs.
- Family Devotionals
  - *Faith Builder Catechism: Devotions to Level Up Your Family Discipleship* – Faith Builder Catechism is a fifty-two-week devotional that helps families press pause on screen time and develop healthy discipleship rhythms in a fun, interactive format. It includes fun stickers so kids can "level up" and track their progress at each stage.[7]

- *Comforting Hearts, Teaching Minds: Family Devotions Based on the Heidelberg Catechism* – This book of daily readings provides a year of family devotions and six to twelve meditations on the main points of each section.[8]
- *Training Hearts, Teaching Minds: Family Devotions Based on the Shorter Catechism* – Similar to the book above, *Training Hearts, Teaching Minds* provides a year of family devotions and six to twelve meditations on the main points of each section.[9]

• Podcast Episode
- *Cross Formed Kidmin* – We cohost this podcast with Ryan Coatney and recorded an entire episode about catechisms. Listen to Episode 22, "Catechisms: The Game Changer for Your Children's Ministry," on your preferred podcast platform.[10]

Hymns

Music is one of the most powerful teaching devices God has created. That's why one of the longest books in the Bible (the Psalms) is a collection of songs and poetry. Songs ingrain ideas into our memory because the words, coupled with music, create an emotional connection that our minds hold on to and cherish. Just think back to your time in church as a kid. What songs come to mind? Some of us remember kids' songs like "Jesus Loves Me" and "My God Is So Big." Others remember hymns such as "Amazing Grace" and "How Great Thou Art."

Consider the songs you sing with your children today. How many are hymns? These timeless songs should be sung and treasured, not because they're old but because they're rich in theology and biblical language. While there are modern worship songs that present excellent doctrine, finding music that replicates the beauty and precision of hymns is rare. Worship songs should be clear and precise in their language about God's nature and work. Vagueness has to be avoided, especially when choosing music for corporate settings. To be clear, we're not discarding new music, but we believe that rejecting hymns due to their age dismisses their proven track record for declaring and retaining God's truth.

There was a season in my life when I experienced job loss and health issues. During this challenging time, hymns from my childhood served as "stones of help" to help me keep my gaze on Christ and find peace in the storm. One of those hymns was "Be Still My Soul." It had been years since I heard that song, but as I was driving from my doctor's appointment and stressing over the need for a job, these words began to flood my mind:

> Be still my soul; the Lord is on thy side;
> bear patiently the cross of grief or pain.
> Leave to thy God to order and provide;
> in every change He faithful will remain.
> Be still my soul; thy best, thy heavenly Friend
> through thorny ways leads to a joyful end.[11]

I remember tearing up as I rehearsed the words in my mind. My life was changing drastically, but I was reminded that God remains faithful and constant. When I got home, I looked up the words to the rest of the hymn and sang the following stanza with confidence and hope:

> Be still, my soul; thy God doth undertake
> to guide the future as He has the past.
> Thy hope, thy confidence let nothing shake;
> all now mysterious shall be bright at last.
> Be still, my soul; the waves and winds still know
> His voice who ruled them while He dwelt below.

God has been our help in ages past. If he can control the wind and the waves and secure the salvation of mankind, surely he is in control of my circumstances. This hymn brought hope because it elevated my gaze to God's power, love, and constancy. What a gift! Hymns like these can serve as gifts to our children as well.

Here are some resources to help you introduce or expose your kids to these beautiful songs of the faith:

- Kingdom Kids Worship: This ministry writes worship music for children that is rich and accessible. They have resources for Scripture, psalms, hymns, and more.
- *The Gospel Story Hymnal*: This book is designed to help parents and leaders pass on stories and hymns of the faith. It includes 150 hymns along with thoughtful notes on scriptural themes, theological concepts, and ideas for living out the faith.[12]
- *Getty Kids Hymnal*: Modern hymn writers Keith and Kristyn Getty have a collection of albums and resources that help teach old and new hymns to the next generation.[13]

The Practice: Map Out Your Pathway

So far, we've looked at the danger of choosing a ministry pathway solely based on its newness or novelty. We presented better criteria for evaluating teaching methodologies that assess potential paths through the filter of a well-structured vision, mission, and philosophy. We also surveyed key biblical passages on teaching kids and highlighted the recurring themes of declaration and retention through Scripture. Then, we suggested tried-and-true pathways the church has used for centuries that declare God's truth and help kids retain it throughout their lives. Now, we're putting it all together by helping you map out the pathway of your children's ministry.

Measure your progress

Vagueness frustrates vision. You cannot hope to get your kids to their destination if you don't have a way to gauge their progress. This is why hiking trails have markers to guide travelers along their routes. If you've ever gone hiking on a public trail, you've seen trail blazes (or markers) painted on trees and rocks. The different colors and symbols not only keep hikers on the right path but also help hikers gauge their distance and progress on the trail. Without these markers, hikers could get lost, discouraged, or hurt. Similarly, if we want kids to thrive in our ministries, we must provide our teachers with spiritual markers that keep them on track, enthusiastic, and consistent.

What should these spiritual markers look like? It will vary from church to church, but here are a starting point and some categories to guide you.

First, you want to start with your goal and work backward. Let's say your goal is to make kids lifelong followers of Christ. Working backward, you would then ask, "What do I believe kids need to learn, do, and experience to follow Christ for a lifetime?" Under each category, you would then write everything you think is necessary for making your goal a reality.

Under the category "Learn," you might write down things such as the basics of the gospel, the Ten Commandments, the Apostles' Creed, the Lord's Prayer, the attributes of God, the books of the Bible, the importance of the church, and so on. Once you have written down what kids need to learn, you move on to the actions and experiences connected to each one.

Under the "Do" category, you might write things such as "trust the gospel"; "memorize certain Bible verses, creeds, or catechism questions," "pray," "read the Bible," "share their testimonies," etc.

After you have compiled a list of what your kids should know and do, list the experiences that foster those ideas and actions. Experiences such as baptism, receiving a Bible, gathering for corporate worship, singing, greeting, serving alongside families in community service projects, attending special classes or events, and so on can be included.

Once you have listed everything you desire your kids to have learned, done, and experienced when it is time for them to graduate from your children's ministry, you can map out how and when they will learn, do, and experience them.

For example, if you want your kids to have memorized the books of the Bible, you'll need to decide when and how you expect them to have all sixty-six books memorized. If you choose to have your kids learn the books of the Bible before leaving elementary school, that becomes a marker on your pathway. Once it's set, you can consider the best approach for helping your kids reach that goal. You could start every Sunday school class by reviewing the books of the Bible, or you could incorporate a "books of the Bible" song during large group teaching.

You can fill in the rest of the map by following the same pattern. Pick a concept, story, or doctrine you believe is necessary for your kids to learn before aging out of your ministry, set a marker for when children should know it, and then incorporate the best actions and experiences to help them reach that marker. That's how you build a map for your pathway!

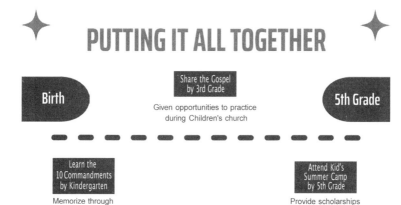

Figure 5. Children's Ministry Pathway Example

Evaluate your strategy

We all have good ideas, but here is where we moderns have gotten off the path. We have lost the ability to monitor the success of our process. We have gotten so obsessed over how many kids are coming that perhaps we have forgotten to ask, "Who are the kids becoming?"

After you have developed the pathway for teaching your kids, you need to set up times to evaluate its effectiveness. Whether this be biannually, annually, or every few years, you need to establish a time to sit with fellow leaders and parents to assess if your pathway is fruitful. Are kids hitting the spiritual markers that have been laid out for them? Do you have realistic goals for what you want them to know, do, and experience and the timeframe in which you hope this to be accomplished? Without consistent, honest evaluation, your pathway could be leading kids to undesired outcomes and frustrations.

Execute your plan

Historically, kids were required to memorize statements of faith, creeds, and important Scripture passages and recite them to confirm their faith in front of the congregation and to qualify as for membership in the church. In our desire to make the path more expansive, we have lost one of the essential aspects of discipleship. A foundation of truth at a young age will influence how that child lives and measures every decision. Because we have not held to a measurable foundation of biblical and historical truth, our kids have only their unanchored experience to guide them in the storms of life.

Solving this problem through a process of instruction requires a systematic approach. Kids don't learn creeds by accident. What we have demonstrated is not meant to be prescriptive but to foster thought and conversation and possibly inspire you to add pieces of what we have done to the pathway you design for your own ministry.

Here is an example of the pathway my (Sam's) church uses.

Preschool

In preschool, we want our kids to know that the church is full of friends to play with, adults who care, and a God who loves them. We introduce them to the idea of structured classes in preschool. We have a Bible story and an activity. The only element of the pathway we use for this age is one *New City Catechism* question a month. We also use a curriculum that puts the bottom line in a question-and-answer format set to song.

We also encourage parents of kids this age to do family worship at home. For kids that are preschool-aged, family worship should be around fifteen minutes in total. This should include reading half of a chapter from the Bible, singing a hymn from YouTube together, and a short one-sentence prayer from each child, with Mom or Dad concluding the time of worship in prayer.

Elementary

In elementary, we want kids to understand that they are more sinful than they know and more loved than they could ever imagine. We want them to understand that God created a perfect world. We broke it, but Jesus redeems it.

We focus more on memorization at this stage than in preschool, although that doesn't mean that other important elements, such as discussion or service, become unimportant. We have a weekly memory verse as well as a weekly catechism question from *The New City Catechism*. We also focus specifically on one of the core elements of the Heidelberg Catechism, so, each year, we have the elementary kids memorize either the Ten Commandments, the Apostles' Creed, the Lord's Prayer, or the books of the Bible. In the month of December, the kids are required over the course of that month to recite back to their small-group leader the section they have been committing to memory (the Lord's Prayer, the Apostles' Creed, the Ten Commandments, or the books of the Bible) and receive whatever the incentive is for that particular year or module. Finally, we write our own VBS curriculum so that we can focus on a different aspect of the Heidelberg Catechism each year. Over a four-year period, we focus on guilt, grace, and gratitude (an overview of the Heidelberg Catechism), the Ten Commandments, the Lord's Prayer, and the Apostles' Creed. We also use a curriculum that puts the bottom line in a question-and-answer format set to song.

We also encourage parents to practice family worship at home. For kids that are in elementary school, family worship should be fifteen minutes but can be extended if good questions come from the reading of Scripture. The format should be the same, except for elementary kids, a full chapter from the Bible is read. You don't have to be a trained scholar to expound the Scripture for your kids. Read it and explain it to the best of your abilities. A great book that helps families learn how to do this is *The Family Worship Bible Guide* by Joel Beeke. It summarizes each chapter in the Bible in a way that is understandable to kids and faithful to the text.

The family should also sing a hymn from YouTube together. The reason for the singing of hymns is that they have been vetted over time, and the classic hymns that remain are typically biblically rich and theologically deep. Family worship should end with a time of prayer that can vary to keep it from becoming too formulaic. Some ways to do this that I have found helpful are reading written prayers from books like *Every Moment Holy*, or praying for the person to their immediate right, or assigning someone to pray for everyone that night. Or you can take requests and can have each member pray for one of the requests. There is no wrong way to pray. *The New City Catechism* asks: "What is prayer?" The answer is "pouring out your heart to God." As long as you are doing that, you are OK. My petition to you is to use variety because if you are coming to God in faith with humility and sincerity, there is no wrong way to pray, and your kids need to see that.

Middle school and high school

At this age, we want our kids to understand the gospel and how the gospel interacts with their daily lives. We also want kids this age to see the value of a group of local believers and to desire to be a part of the church.

In our middle school and high school meetings, we cover a weekly *New City Catechism* question—the same one that we cover in our kids' church environments. On Sunday mornings, our high school students attend the weekend church service with our adults. Our middle school students leave after we sing songs, and we do a discipleship class during the sermon. In that discipleship class, we cover *The New City Catechism, Pilgrim's Progress*, and biblical theology.

Both middle school students and high school students are encouraged to take part in our yearly memorization program, where students are challenged to memorize the entire New City Catechism, as well as memorize whole books of the Bible, learn the names of all the books of the Bible, and learn the Ten Commandments, the Apostles' Creed, and the Lord's Prayer. Those who do this are tested and typically receive an incentive for completing the challenge.

College

At this age, we want young adults to understand the gospel and have a gospel framework for viewing everything. We want them to not only understand the gospel but to apply it in every context in which they find themselves.

For this group, we offer a part-time internship that includes discipleship, Bible reading, accountability, and serving in the church, as well as a weekday evening classroom setting where we explicitly walk through systematic theology in the fall semester and through biblical worldview topics and issues in the spring semester.

Our hope is that what kids learn is systematic, holistic, and corroborative of what they already know to be true. Again, this isn't a perfect plan, and some of it may work for you, while some of it may not. I do hope it helps you think about how we can disciple our kids and train them using historical, biblical, and theological practices. Our kids and our parents need us to think deeply about how we provide opportunities to know God and be known by him.

As our good friend Ryan Coatney says, "Discipleship is never an accident"—it requires our participation, our planning, and our effort—"but it's always a miracle." The fact that our kids come to see Jesus as beautiful in the end is the greatest miracle of all. We plant and water, and God makes things grow. As you develop your pathway, trust the promise of Philippians 1:6. He who began a good work in you (and the kids in your ministry) will bring it to completion at the day of Jesus Christ.

DISCUSSION QUESTIONS

1. Does your church/ministry have a clearly defined vision, mission, and philosophy? If not, use the questions in this chapter to work with your leadership to craft them. If so, honestly evaluate your ministry to see if your vision, mission, and philosophy serve as the criteria for everything done within it.

2. Scripture presents "declaration and retention" as the primary means by which God's people are to teach theology to the next generation. Does your ministry thrive in both? Is there one that needs more work? Have you replaced one or both with other methods (for example: entertainment and attention)?

3. Several tried-and-true pathways for teaching were presented in this chapter. Are there any you are currently utilizing? Are there any you wish to implement? Why or why not?

4. To teach kids fruitfully, a ministry's path needs to be mapped out. We have provided a template in Appendix 3 to aid you in creating a map of your ministry's pathway.

Chapter 8

Bringing Theology Home

During my first cross-country race, I (Hunter) learned the hard way that *how* you train is just as important as *what* you train. I joined the team late and assumed that my experience playing other sports would be enough to carry me through. I had been running during the time leading up to the race, but my training was inconsistent. When race day came, I took off like a rocket at the start and was well ahead of the pack for the first mile, but soon got winded and began slowing down. My sprint turned into a run, then a jog, and ultimately into a defeated walk. My poor performance made it embarrassingly apparent that my training did not match the kind of race I was running.

THE PROBLEM: OUTSOURCING DISCIPLESHIP

The biblical authors often use the analogy of a race to describe the Christian life. Believers are called to run toward Christ with endurance (Hebrews 12:1). The Christian life is a spiritual race of endurance, and if we want our kids to run the race of faith well, then we need to train them in the correct manner. Since discipleship is a marathon and not a sprint, the training we offer not only needs to have the right content but also the right consistency.

While this book is primarily aimed at church leaders and volunteers, we recognize that individuals can only do so much. A child's time in children's ministry is limited. There are 168 hours in a week, and at best, a church will have a child in their ministry environment for one or two hours a week. That's roughly 1 percent of their time! Imagine if athletes only had a 1 percent training rate for their sport. They would be terrible! In saying this, we're not neglecting the power of and need for the local church in a child's life, but we have to recognize the limitations that the local church has timewise. Just as an athlete or musician can't practice an hour a week and expect to master their sport or instrument, neither should a church expect their kids to thrive spiritually by attending a children's ministry or Sunday school class a couple of times a month. If we want our kids to run the race set before them with endurance, then we need to give them consistent training. Such training is only possible when the church partners with parents.

Beyond the stalemate

In the introduction of this book, we referenced a research project called *Children's Ministry in a New Reality*. One of the primary findings of this study is what the Barna Group and Awana call "the stalemate." What's the stalemate? Children's ministry leaders, churched adults, and parents were asked where the primary source of discipleship should be. 95 percent of children's ministry leaders say the home should be primary, but churched adults and parents aren't so sure. Both groups are almost split down the middle on the primary domain of discipleship for children. With approximately 50 percent thinking the primary domain is the church and the others thinking the primary domain is the home, the conversation would appear to be in a stalemate. Both parties seem stuck with no apparent progress.[1]

While the stalemate between parents and churched adults is concerning, there's another potential issue hiding within these statistics. If 95 percent of children's ministry leaders claim to see the home as the primary domain of discipleship, why do only 50 percent of parents agree? If most kids' ministry leaders champion families, the number of parents who believe they are the primary disciple makers should be higher. The statistics don't seem to match up.

We're not claiming ministry leaders are being dishonest in their responses. We meet with children's pastors regularly and consistently hear them promote the primacy of parents in child discipleship. We believe the disconnect is not in their claims but in their practice.

> Most children's ministry leaders may be consistent in their belief that parents are the primary disciple makers, but many are inconsistent in their practice of equipping families to live it out.

That last sentence may sound like an assumption or condemnation, but it's neither. From our conversations with children's pastors and volunteers, the majority quickly admit they don't know how to connect with and equip families effectively. When families feel ill-equipped to fulfill their calling, they're more prone to outsource their child's discipleship to the "professionals." As we've shown throughout this book, ministry leaders have an incredible responsibility to study, teach, and live out sound doctrine before their kids, but this should be done in partnership with families, not apart from them.

Rethinking education

The struggle to partner with families could be tied to how education is perceived in the United States. Ninety percent of US children attend public school, making its model the de facto reference point for education among parents and leaders.[2] In this model, parents send their kids to institutions where they are taught various subjects among their peers in the community. Teachers in these schools are seen as primary, with parents providing supplemental guidance and accountability.

In the statements above, we're not trying to present anything positive or negative about the public school system, but we want to recognize the impact its model can have on our understanding of how children are taught in the church.

With kids being sent to professionals for schooling, parents can adopt a similar mindset when it comes to spiritual formation. They might send their kids to the "professionals" at church to teach them the basics of the faith and intuitively think this is the whole of their child's spiritual training. Church leaders can adopt this mindset as well and unknowingly structure their ministries to operate much like a public school setting. This could explain the disconnect ministry leaders experience with equipping families. Ministry leaders may believe that parents are the primary disciple makers, but their experience with the dominant educational system hasn't provided them with a framework to empower discipleship in the home. Sending kids to a Sunday school or children's ministry class isn't the primary discipling moment of their week. The teaching that takes place in these settings is the starting point and provides parents with the content needed to train their kids throughout the week. It's the opposite of the public-school model, which is why it feels counterintuitive.

Again, we're not knocking the system, but if we want to train our children to know the truth and run toward Christ with unwavering resolve, we need our system of training to match the race they are running. We need to look beyond educational trends and tap into the design God has provided his people for teaching children.

THE PRINCIPLE: THEOLOGICAL TRAINING IS A PARTNERSHIP

The kids we serve won't be theologically fluent if they aren't trained consistently, and consistent training most effective when church leaders partner with parents to continue their discipleship at home. "Partnership" is the key word because parents and local churches need one another to adequately fulfill the Great Commission. Parents need the community and guidance of the local church, and ministry leaders need the commitment and consistency of parents. Without the local church, theological training from parents would be lacking, and without parents, theological training from the local church would be limited. Both are needed for robust, holistic discipleship. Scripture speaks highly of both sides of the partnership:

- Local Church - Parents = Theological Training That Is Limited
- Parents - Local Church = Theological Training That Is Lacking

God has elected the church to be the pillar and buttress, or foundation, for truth (1 Timothy 3:15) and has established leaders within it to equip the saints (parents included) for the work of the ministry, which is to build up the body of Christ (Ephesians 4:11–12). Parents will struggle to be the disciple makers they're called to be if they're not under the authority and teaching of a biblically faithful church. They need a steady diet of sound teaching, so they, in turn, can have a sturdy foundation on which to build their leadership of their kids. Parents need the wisdom of ministry leaders and older saints to give them godly instruction on how to love well, show integrity, and live faithfully for God (Titus 2:1–6).

On the flip side, God has designed the family to be a hub of faith formation. Parents are to acquaint their children with the writings of Scripture from a young age (2 Timothy 3:14–15) and bring them up in the discipline and instruction of the Lord (Ephesians 6:4). They are to diligently teach their children on a consistent basis by speaking of God at all times, in all places, and in all situations (Deuteronomy 6:4–9). It's clear that both church leaders and parents are called to teach children the truths of God and need each other to do so fruitfully. The million-dollar question is: What should this partnership look like?

Empowerment

Empowerment is a combination of encouragement and equipping. Parents need to be encouraged in their God-given role and equipped to live it out faithfully. Both are needed. Encouragement without equipping can lead to fruitlessness, and equipping without encouragement can lead to frustration.

Encouraging parents requires constant reminders and proofs of concept. We need to remind parents through teaching, conversations, emails, and messages that they have been chosen by God to disciple their children. Along with Scripture, we can share stories and statistics that demonstrate the power of God's design for the family. In the book *Handing Down the Faith*, Christian Smith and Amy Adamczyk detail the reasons why parents are the key players in spiritual formation. They say, "All research in the United States today shows clearly that parents are by far the most important factor influencing their children's religion, not only as youth but also after they leave home."[3] Parents have the greatest amount of time and the largest number of mechanisms for handing down the faith to their kids. The families in our churches need to be shown this type of research from time to time to realize that their role as disciple makers is more than a nice concept. It's real, and it really works.

In addition to encouragement, families need to know they're not alone. They might be primary in their child's discipleship, but they're not solitary. We need to give them a framework for spiritual formation in the home, along with the tools to make it happen. Many books have been written on the topic of family discipleship, and more resources exist for families to train their kids than ever before. How can you ensure the resources you provide for your families are best? Whatever type of resources you provide, it needs to be accessible, doable, and measurable.

Accessible

Accessibility helps you answer this question: How easy is it for families to understand and access what I'm encouraging them to do? If the framework you provide for your families is too complicated or if the resources are too difficult to access, the equipping will fail before it gets started. Optimizing accessibility requires us to ponder and answer the following questions:

- How will I help families understand the nature of family discipleship? Will it come through meetings, training sessions, or online classes?
- What resources do we provide for families to disciple their kids at home? Does our curriculum include such resources? Do we want/need to create our own?
- How do we make these resources available to them? Do we have a recommended resource wall or table at the church? Do we have a website page or social media group that families can go to for suggestions and frequently asked questions?

Doable

Doable discipleship answers this question: How easy is it for families to accomplish what I'm encouraging them to do? Your training and equipping can be understandable and easy to access, but if it isn't doable, it doesn't matter. Discipleship doesn't have to be hard to be meaningful. We should be providing families with clear, easy-to-follow pathways of discipleship in the home. Our suggested pathways should be scalable, meaning that more steps, details, and depth can be added, depending on the age and maturity of those being discipled. To do this well, you need to ask questions and do things like these:

- What is the goal of family discipleship, and what can I give my families to help them reach that goal?
- For example, the goal for your families might be increased levels of biblical literacy. In this case, a doable step for your families would be giving them a Bible engagement plan that is easy to implement and accomplish.
- Or, if the goal is learning the basics of the faith, give your families access to a catechism and provide a weekly plan to work through and memorize.

Measurable

You can give your families an accessible, doable discipleship framework for the home, but is it effective? Is it accomplishing its purpose for your families? Being measurable answers this question: How easy is it to test the fruitfulness of what I'm encouraging my families to do? This question is important but can easily get confused with being doable. Just because a family can do what you've offered them doesn't mean that it's fruitful. You need to measure the use of your resources and see if they are effective. You can do this by asking questions and considering points like these:

- What outcomes should the framework and resources I've provided for my families produce? What difference should I expect to see in our families' knowledge, behavior, and priorities as a result of our equipping?

- How can I best align the discipleship pathway of my ministry with the pathways of discipleship in the home? (See chapter 7 for a review of pathways.) This could be the easiest way to gauge effectiveness. Instead of seeing family discipleship as a separate thing in your ministry, see it as an integral part of accomplishing your ministry.
- For example, if a marker on your discipleship pathway is to memorize specific Scripture passages, then equip families with suggested rhythms and resources for memorizing those passages at home. The more the church and family discipleship pathways can overlap, the easier it will be to make the equipping you provide accessible, doable, and measurable.

To summarize, God has designed families and churches to partner together in the theological training of their kids. To do this well, churches need to empower parents to consistently disciple kids in their homes. Empowering families requires encouragement and equipping, and equipping needs to be accessible, doable, and measurable if it is to be fruitful. With that said, we now turn to the practice, and we provide categories for helping your families point to Christ in all that they do.

THE PRACTICE: POINT TO CHRIST IN ALL THINGS

The goal of parenting is not perfection but to be a faithful undershepherd of the Great Shepherd. We must point kids relentlessly to their True North. This next section will discuss practical ways ministry leaders can help parents pass on their faith to the next generation. Before we get started in the practical ways to do this, I have put together a few reminders that I (Sam) often share with our parents at baby dedications and in family counseling:

- *Be the same person at home and at church.* One of the most extraordinary things parents can do is not try to be perfect but to point to a perfect Savior. When parents point to Christ at home, in the car, at the grocery store, and everywhere in between, it shows their kids that Jesus is worth following at all times and in every circumstance.

- *Suffer publicly.* The things that cause us pain reveal what is most valuable to us. The person to whom (or thing to which) parents turn in times of sorrow and pain will show their kids who or what operates as their functional saviors. Inviting parents to evaluate the pain points in their lives and where they run to for hope can help them suffer well in front of their kids. The call to discipleship is a call to take up our crosses daily. This means suffering is a part of the plan. As parents, everything we do should point beyond ourselves to Christ. Our kids must learn from our example that we do things for God because our hearts have been saved by grace alone. Suffering is one of those things. Facing difficulty does not make us better than any other Christian; trusting Jesus in the middle of the storm is exactly what Christ modeled for us on the cross.

- *Be gospel-centered leaders.* Grace creates transparent leaders in two ways: it convinces us that we are loved with unbreakable and unyielding affection and compels us to own up to the manifold ways we reject such love. We often look for principles to help us lead better and love more. Gospel-centered leaders are not just practitioners of gospel principles; they also live lives marked by repentance. Pastor Matt Adair concurs: "Beyond our principles and practices, gospel-centered leadership models a life of repentance and faith."[4] Help parents see that being older and having more life experience won't make them perfect. Occasions will arise when they need to repent to their kids for the ways in which they have not honored Christ in their behavior and decisions.

- *Trust Jesus completely.* While it is the job of parents to model a life of faith to their kids, they are powerless to save them. Only Christ can save them. We water, we plant, but God makes things grow. This is true of plants and even more true of our kids' hearts.
- *Pray without ceasing.* Our first instinct as parents must be prayer. Prayer is pouring our hearts out to God. It is the most profoundly helpful way we can reorient ourselves in the craziness of raising our kids. Prayer is a practical way to remind ourselves that God is God, and we are not. He alone has the power to save.

Normal trumps novel

Our culture leads us to believe that if something isn't novel, then it isn't impactful. But this couldn't be further from the truth! The ordinary, not the exceptional, is what shapes us the most. Consider smooth stones in a calm creek. They aren't shaped by sporadic blasts of water but by a gentle, consistent stream of water over time. Our children are shaped in the same way. We need to help parents in our churches see the formative power of consistency and the big changes that can occur in their children through small habits over time.

For example, parents who engage in prayer or Scripture reading for a few minutes a day will find that that habit can be more formative than long sessions of family worship held inconsistently. Habits reveal priorities and ingrain those priorities into our hearts.

Adding new habits can be intimidating to many families, but it doesn't need to be. You can help your families own their schedules and establish faith-forming habits by using "habit stacking." This concept, articulated by James Clear, makes adding habits easier by attaching them to existing ones. Habit stacking begins by observing your week and determining existing habits—habits such as driving kids to school, eating dinner together, bedtime routines, etc. After families have listed out their current habits, they can then stack spiritual habits on top of them.

For example, if a mom drives her kids to school every day, she can use the time in the car to play Scripture memory songs or review catechisms with her kids. Or, if a family has dinner at home every Monday, Wednesday, and Friday, they can use those mealtimes to read Scripture or a story from a storybook Bible. Families can also add prayers of supplication during bedtime routines or prayers of thanksgiving on the way home from sports practices. The options are endless, but we need to give our families the framework and tools to see their schedules as a string of habits on which they can stack spiritual habits.

Habit stacking isn't a new concept. It's what Moses had in mind in Deuteronomy 6 when he told families to teach children about the commands of God when they woke up, went to bed, and walked along the road. Teaching theology was never posited as a novel thing but as a normal experience of everyday life. Normal moments trump novel experiences in the theological training of our children.

For more tips and ideas on the use of habits in discipleship, check out the book *Habits of the Household* by Justin Whitmel Earley (Zondervan 2021).

Conversations (the secret sauce)

Part of making theological training normal is making it less formal. As we shared in chapter 2, our definitions of theology determine how we approach and teach it. Since many parents see theology as studious or academic, they might think they have to teach it formally to teach it correctly. But, as we've explained, this isn't the case. Everyone is a theologian, including every parent, and there isn't a moment that goes by in which parents aren't doing and teaching theology. We need to help parents see their role as theologians and empower them to speak good theology fluently.

The research in *Handing Down the Faith* says that one of the most formational things parents do in passing down their faith is having consistent spiritual conversations with their children:

> Religious language is not mainstream Americans' first language; it is a second language at best. So learning to believe and practice a religion requires essentially learning a second language, and that always requires practice talking, even when one is surrounded by native speakers. When parents regularly talk with children about religious matters in ordinary conversational settings, that provides children with exactly the kind of sustained practice in learning the second language that is necessary for religion to be sensible.[5]

The focus on conversational settings is worth noting. A conversation is informal. It doesn't have a strict structure, talking points, or handouts. It ebbs and flows and leans heavily on improvisation. Teaching theology through conversation means taking the elements of everyday life and discussion and directing them toward Christ.

One day, my (Hunter's) daughter Margot lost a tiny toy that was precious to her. She cried in a panic, thinking it would remain lost forever. In a God-given moment, I thought to ask, "Do you think God knows where it is?" Through the tears, Margot said, "Yeah, he knows where everything is." I followed up her answer with an invitation: "Since God knows where it is, he might help us find it. Let's pray and ask God to help us see where it is." After we prayed, Margot found the toy within five minutes. No joke! It was a pretty cool moment and became a memory she references often. I would have missed this precious experience if I hadn't turned the conversation about a lost toy toward God's omniscience.

As a side note, these moments don't always pan out so smoothly. My son, Clarke, was also present when God answered my prayer to find Margot's toy, so when he lost one of his favorite toy cars a few months later, he asked me to pray that God would help us find it. After praying for a couple of days with no car in sight, Clarke became discouraged and asked me, "Why doesn't God answer my prayers?" I'll be honest. I fumbled for a bit, trying to figure out how to explain why God answered our prayers for Margot's toy and not his. After stuttering and stammering for a response, I decided to focus on what I *did* know instead of what I *didn't* know. I said something to this effect (though not as clearly and concisely). "I don't know why God hasn't helped us find your car, but I do know this. He is good, and always does what is best for us. We know he does what is best for us, because he sent Jesus to live, die, and rise for us. We'll keep praying, but even if we don't find it, remember that every good thing we have is from God. We can trust him no matter what."

In Deuteronomy 6, Moses puts the emphasis on conversations. Wherever families were and whatever they were doing, they were to talk about God's truth (Deuteronomy 6:7). Conversation, no matter the topic, can serve as a catalyst for discipleship. We need to equip families to both look for informal teachable moments and prep for set-aside moments of formal teaching.

Several years ago, one of my (Sam's) kids struggled with lying. The typical response I have given and heard many other parents give is, "Hey, don't tell lies because our family doesn't tell lies." While true, this is a moralistic answer to a theological problem. I admit this was what I was going to say when I first faced this problem with my child. But God, by his grace, reminded me that our identity is not primarily founded in our family or origin but in Christ.

By grace, I responded to my child by telling him that lies are a sin because they separate us from God first and foremost, and they also separate us from those around us. Lies are sins both against God and against other people. I then responded by saying, "Do you know why we most often tell lies?" The answer I got was "no." I said, "Most people tell lies because they are afraid of disappointing someone or want to impress someone." The reason we lie is to preserve love or gain love. When we understand how much we are loved in Christ, we are free to tell the truth because we are already loved.

As parents, we tend to point at our kids in anger or point to ourselves in pride. But gospel-centered parents will see Christ in all events of life and, in humility, point away from themselves and point to Christ. The reality of every human relationship is that it is imperfect. We will fail our kids in some way. We must train them to depend on a Father who will never fail them and who will never leave them; we want them to know that he is a good Father who has sent his Spirit to be with them till the end of the age.

Training the trainers

For parents to be theologically fluent and turn everyday experiences into teachable moments, they need to be immersed in God's truth themselves. The church needs to train and provide parents with tools to grow in their theological competence so they, in turn, can train their children. Here are some suggestions to do that.

Encourage them to pray for wisdom and grace

Parenting is not for the faint of heart, and no matter how prepared and diligent the parents in your church may be, parenting requires mounds of grace. As a leader, you may be tempted to give the families you serve answers and resources for every question they have or problem they face, but where they need to start is in prayer. They must ask God for wisdom for the unique situation they find themselves in. No two kids are the same. There are no formulas or pat answers that will work across the board. Principles, yes, but formulas, no. Few things will remind us of our dependence on God and his great mercy like prayer.

Continually reinforce a love for God's Word

Let me say this: we (the authors of this book) are both avid readers and love books. When parents in our congregations face specific and unique challenges in their parenting and in the discipleship of their own kids, it's very tempting for us to give them a resource rather than point them to Scripture. As a leader who values the Word, you must make sure that everything you do is grounded in and focuses on God's Word, not your good ideas. When we push books and ideas over Scripture, we subtly erode the foundation beneath those very ideas. I love how Deuteronomy 6:4b–5 is so explicitly God centered: "The Lord our God, the Lord is one. You shall love the Lord your God with all your heart and with all your soul and with all your might." This is the foundation for all that follows. We must be faithful to Scripture in our answers to our kids and in our practice as leaders. Scripture must be the lens by which we see the world rather than just another accessory in our parenting toolbox. We beg you—train the parents in your church to value God's Word.

Host training events for families

With the advent of online training and in-person training, we have more avenues to connect with and equip parents. I have seen some churches host in-person miniconferences to reinforce the value of child discipleship, while others have done small groups for parents, and still others have produced online events. You need to assess the needs of the parents in your church and then create a strategy to practically meet those needs. This can happen through conversations with kids, families, and those in the larger church body. What do the parents across your church need? A great way to discover this in a timely fashion is through a survey. Google Forms, SurveyMonkey, and Gloo are all excellent options we have used at different times. Parents need help from you and from other families in your church to know how to effectively disciple their kids. Assessing the need helps you know how to specifically help them at their points of need.

Encourage your pastors to address issues of family and parenting frequently from the pulpit

No one has more time and influence over your parents than your senior leaders. Encourage your pastors to talk about their families and the rhythms of care and discipleship they model in their homes. When the Scripture they are teaching from references parenting, kids, or families, have them stress the values your church has around child discipleship. The influence your pastors have cannot be overstated. I (Sam) remember trying for years to get our families to adopt and use a catechism with their kids. It was only mildly successful until our pastor started using it with his kids and then talked about it from the pulpit. It was a game changer! Have regular conversations with your pastors about how they view child discipleship and give them good resources to be able to use with their kids and recommend to others.

Model for the parents in your church what the proactive discipleship of children looks like

One of the qualifications of godly leaders in 1 Timothy is that they have their houses in order. This is not a demand for perfection but for transparent reinforcement of biblical truth. As a leader, you do not have control over the heart and mind of your children. You are, however, responsible for how you teach them, how you respond to their actions, and how you model Christ to them. Salvation is a work Christ alone does, but he often uses us and, most often, parents in the child's life to model Christ's beauty. As a leader, how you raise and intentionally disciple your kids will speak louder to the parents you are called to train and equip than any event you put on. The orderliness of your kids' lives is usually the result of patience, prayer, and perseverance in the truth. What you tell your parents about family discipleship must also be modeled.

Provide resources for the families in your church

When I first became a kids' pastor in the late nineties, the problem we had was a lack of resources for kid and family discipleship. Today the problem is an issue of curation. There are so many resources available to us now. What we have to do for our families is direct them to quality resources that reflect our churches' values. The resources you provide for them are, in a way, an act of discipleship. You are picking resources that will be forming your parents' hearts and minds in a particular way. Involve your lead pastor and key elders or leaders in the process to make sure that you choose resources that reflect your church's theological framework.

Here are a few resources that we recommend to jump-start your search for theologically rich discipleship materials.

Books

- *Family Discipleship* by Matt Chandler and Adam Griffin
- *Forming Faith: Discipling the Next Generation in a Post-Christian Culture* by Matt Markins, Mike Handler, and Sam Luce
- *Caring for the Souls of Children: A Biblical Counselor's Manual* edited by Amy Baker
- *Talking with Your Kids about God: 30 Conversations Every Christian Parent Must Have* by Natasha Crain
- *Everyday Talk: Talking Freely and Naturally about God with Your Children* by John Younts
- *Discover: Questioning Your Way to Faith* by Mike McGarry

Websites

- GospelCenteredFamily.com
- ChildDiscipleship.com
- Renewanation.org

Podcasts

- *Family Discipleship Podcast*
- *Raising Cross-Formed Kids*
- *Tiny Theologians Podcast*

Hopefully, you've captured the importance of the church-family partnership in discipling kids. One of the best ways to teach kids theology is to teach their parents how to teach them theology. Doing so extends your teaching beyond the walls of the church into the everyday moments of their lives. Partnering with parents better equips kids to run the race of faith set before them and helps them know God more fully. Praise God for his beautiful design of the church and home!

DISCUSSION QUESTIONS

1. Reflect on your own experiences or observations of training and education. How has the analogy of the Christian life as a race resonated with your understanding? Have you ever found yourself, like Hunter, realizing that the manner of your preparation did not align with the challenges you faced?

2. Consider the "stalemate" mentioned regarding the primary domain of discipleship for children, in which 95 percent of children's ministry leaders advocate for the home as the primary source of discipleship, but only 50 percent of parents agree. Why do you think there is this divide? How might children's spiritual development be impacted by parents who do not view their home as the primary domain of discipleship?

3. Reflect on the concept of "habit stacking" mentioned in this chapter. How can this approach be applied in your own life or in the lives of the families you work with to incorporate spiritual habits into daily routines? Can you think of specific habits that could be stacked onto existing ones to foster theological training at home?

4. Consider the importance of conversations in family discipleship. How can informal, everyday conversations serve as a powerful tool for teaching theology? Can you share an experience from your life where a casual conversation led to a meaningful theological insight or revelation?

Remember and Believe— Nothing Else Matters

In *The Silver Chair*, C. S. Lewis lays out how we should train our children and emphasizes the role that theology plays in the life and framework of a child.

At the beginning of the book, the great lion Aslan, who is a type of Christ, gives Jill, a young girl new to Narnia, a quest, but, before he sends her out, he gives her signs and guideposts for her journey: "I will tell you, Child," said the Lion. "These are the signs by which I will guide you in your quest."

Aslan then tells her the signs she must repeat until she can say them perfectly. You might say the lion CATechised Jill (It's OK; I have four kids. Dad jokes are now a requirement.). Once she could say them by heart, Aslan both instructed and warned her:

> Remember, remember, remember the signs. Say them to yourself when you wake in the morning and when you lie down at night, and when you wake in the middle of the night. And whatever strange things may happen to you, let nothing turn your mind from following the signs. And secondly, I give you a warning. Here on the mountain, I have spoken to you clearly: I will not often do so down in Narnia. Here on

the mountain, the air is clear, and your mind is clear; as you drop down into Narnia, the air will thicken. Take great care that it does not confuse your mind. And the signs which you have learned here will not look at all as you expect them to look when you meet them there. That is why it is so important to know them by heart and pay no attention to appearances. Remember the signs and believe the signs. Nothing else matters.[1]

The application of this paragraph was meaningful in Lewis's day and prophetic for our own. There is a clarity and innocence that kids have in their childhood and youth that we must protect. The thin air of the mountain is where our kids are protected from the world, and they see, in our communities of faith and in our families of origin, the beauty of the gospel on full display. But we also must prepare them for the world they will meet. This is where the warning comes in.

The warning is that as our kids grow, the air thickens with the cares of this world. Distractions are everywhere, and what we have invested in the hearts and minds of our kids will not be wasted. Things will not look like they expect them to look, but we are not to be led astray by our emotions or our feelings. We must remind our kids to remember the truths they were taught and to believe in the Person who condescended and modeled for us what those truths look like. We must remind our kids, in an age of distraction, discouragement, and disillusionment, to stay relentlessly focused on Jesus: "Nothing else matters."

As we end our time together, we want to leave you with this final encouragement: what you have been called to do matters more than you realize and more than most people will recognize. It can feel overwhelming. It can be discouraging. Know this: You are not alone.

The author of Hebrews writes to Jewish believers in Christ to remind them and encourage them to stay focused on what matters most. In the midst of difficulties, persecution, and sorrow, the author reminds them that Jesus is better than everything in Judaism, and that they can endure because of the example of those who have gone before them and because of the character of Christ.

> Therefore, since we are surrounded by so great a cloud of witnesses, let us also lay aside every weight, and sin which clings so closely, and let us run with endurance the race that is set before us, looking to Jesus, the founder and perfecter of our faith, who for the joy that was set before him endured the cross, despising the shame, and is seated at the right hand of the throne of God. Consider him who endured from sinners such hostility against himself, so that you may not grow weary or fainthearted. (Hebrews 12:1–3)

Invest your time and energy in theological truths. Impress them on your kids. In a world obsessed with how things look, pay no attention to appearances. "Remember the signs and believe the signs. Nothing else matters."

Do not grow weary. Do not shrink back. Look to Jesus. We endure not because we are strong runners, but because we have a beautiful Savior.

Our desire is that this book becomes a tool that instructs you and empowers you to take God's Word seriously. Your kids will never see the beauty of Christ or the loveliness of Christian doctrine if you don't find Christ and his teachings beautiful. We also desire that this book acts as a warning. The need for depth and richness of theological truths in our children's ministries and churches has never been more necessary. It is not something we can ignore in our day and hope for the best. It is necessary that we understand our times and know that the answer to those times is not political activism or spiritual pessimism—it is a robust understanding of what is true and what has always been true.

Our hope is that this book serves as a foundation and catalyst for a lifelong pursuit of the depths of God's Word, and then as a catalyst for sharing those words with the children God has placed in our care. St. Jerome is believed to have said, "The Scriptures are shallow enough for a babe to come and drink without fear of drowning and deep enough for a theologian to swim in without ever touching the bottom." This is our prayer: that you will swim in the depths of God's Word so that the children whom God has placed in your care can fearlessly come and drink. In Christ, they will develop both a thirst that can only be satisfied by God and a taste for what is truly good, truly true, and truly beautiful.

Bible Lesson Prep Sheet

STUDY THE PASSAGE

Context, content, Christ, and consequence

This simple method will help you study a biblical passage or story so that you can consult Scripture thoughtfully and compare it to the teaching found within your curriculum.

Context
- Ask contextual questions such as "Who?" "What?" "When?" "Where?" and "Why?"
- You might ask, "Who wrote this passage, and to whom was it written? When was it written? Where does this passage take place? What took place before this passage? Why was this passage written?"

Content
- Content refers to the truth your passage intends to teach about God and all things in relation to him.
- Answer the "God question": What is happening in this passage, and what does it reveal about God? What does it reveal about his nature, character, and works in our world, and what does that reveal about us?

Christ
- Here are four questions you can ask that build bridges to Christ in every story you tell from Scripture:

1. How do I teach this passage in a distinctively Christian way?[1]
2. What aspect of the gospel is shown in this story?[2]
3. How does God accomplish the same thing— only better—in Jesus?[3]
4. Who in this story needs the good news?[4]

Consequence
- How should the content of this passage change our lives?
- Are there prayers that need to be prayed? Are there sins that need to be confessed? Are there promises that need to be kept? Are there actions that need to be taken? Are there words that need to be spoken? Are there thoughts that need to be changed?

UTILIZE THE FLOWER TECHNIQUE

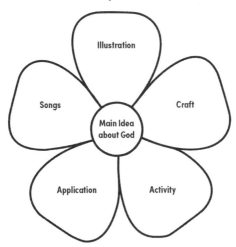

As you prepare to teach a lesson to the kids in your class, you need to ask yourself, "What is the bottom line? What is the one idea I'm trying to get across? What is the one thing I want my kids to remember from this lesson?" The big idea or bottom line should always be about God in some way.

- Once you have determined the main idea about God from your passage, choose teaching elements that flow out of and reinforce the main idea. In order to determine the main idea and know what teaching elements to choose, you will need to have studied the passage and answered the questions under the headings above (Context, Content, Christ, and Consequence).
- Memorize the key message so that you can repeat it more often than the curriculum does.
- Plan out how you are going to communicate what you have studied to the kids in your class. Your goal is for them to understand and remember, so you need to put it on their level.

APPLY DOCTRINE FROM SCRIPTURE

To see the practical implications of a doctrine, we need to identify what a particular passage or truth teaches about God and everything in relation to him.

When studying a passage or doctrines, ask these simple questions:

- How does this truth about God change the way I think about *myself*?
- How does this truth about God change the way I think about *others*?
- How does this truth about God change the way I think about the *world*?

As you study, you could formulate the practical application by filling in the blanks below:

- How does the truth about _____ (insert doctrine) change the way I think about _____ (insert sphere of life)?

Read through the story or the lesson at least four times. The more you read it, the better, as you will be able to personalize it by adding stories or examples from your life and internalize the content so that you can deliver the lesson without having to read the entire lesson to your kids.

Conclude your study with prayer. There is something powerful about acknowledging our need for the Holy Spirit's help in our lesson preparation and in applying what we have learned.

Example Lesson: Distilling the Doctrine of Sin

Many kids' ministry curricula fail to address the topic of sin, and the ones that do often oversimplify the concept, which results in children not understanding their need for God's help. Below, we have included a complete lesson plan that features distillation throughout. It does not shy away from using complex words (when necessary) but explains them in a way that children can understand. The lesson does not merely mention sin in a generic way but instead presents God as a personal being who is both loving and just.

Below you will notice that I left out Exodus 32:15–29. The reason I did so is because you will probably have difficulty teaching thirty-five verses to kids in eight to ten minutes. The reason I focused on the verses I did is because they contain the main point of the text. The catechism tells us the purpose of the law is to reveal the sinful nature of man, the holy nature of God, and thus our need for a Savior. In this chapter, we see the sinful nature of man on full display (creation and worship of a false god), the holy nature of God (his just desire to destroy sinful man), the need for a Savior (on display in the role of Moses as a mediator and God as gracious Redeemer), and Moses here pointing forward to the present ministry of

Jesus for us. Talking with kids about broken tablets and the ground-up gold they were forced to drink has helpful aspects but would have distracted from the core message of this text when you have eight to ten minutes to teach a room of kids ranging from five to ten years old.

GUILT OF SIN

Memory Verse: "For by grace you have been saved through faith. And this is not your own doing; it is the gift of God, not a result of works, so that no one may boast." Ephesians 2:8–9

Guilt – Adam's sin, our sin, Jesus's solution

- **Bible Story – Exodus 32:1–14, 30–35**
  – What is the gospel?
  – The purpose of law—it shows us we are guilty.
  – By making the golden calf, the Israelites were breaking the first commandment as it was being given.
- **Catechism – Question #15** Since no one can keep the law, what is its purpose?
  Answer: That we may know the holy nature and will of God, and the sinful nature and disobedience of our hearts; and thus our need of a Savior. The law also teaches and exhorts us to live a life worthy of our Savior.

  Bottom Line - We can't keep God's law perfectly. Jesus kept it for us, and helps us keep it by the Spirit. And now, with the Spirit's help, we can grow in joyfully obeying God's law out of gratitude for his grace.

LEADER LESSON

Distillation of the Doctrine of Sin:

For kids to understand sin properly, they must understand that sin is a particular thing. The Westminster Confession states, "Every sin, both original and actual, being a transgression of the righteous law of God . . . "[1] For kids to understand sin, we must establish the basis for our understanding in Scripture. We must show that sin is not something that happens to us; it is something we are born into. Because we are descended from Adam and Eve, who were our first parents, we received the consequence of their sin and the same nature and ability to commit sins of our own. As a result, we sin and break God's laws daily, on purpose and on accident. The question regarding our sin is, "What do kids need to know about sin?" I believe they need to know three things:

1. The nature of our sin and the greatness of our sin.
2. The nature of our forgiveness and help.
3. The response of gratitude that should come naturally from someone who has received forgiveness and has found life and joy in Christ.

LARGE GROUP

Bible Story: The Golden Calf - Exodus 32

Intro:

Hey everyone, welcome back to kids' church. Over the next few weeks, we are going to be talking about how we can look at the Bible and understand what Jesus did for us through three key words: Guilt, Grace, and Gratitude. Today we are going to look at that first word—guilt. Our bottom line for this morning is this: **We can't keep God's law**

perfectly, so Jesus kept it for us. The main thing that we have to know and remember is that we are all guilty of breaking God's law.

I have up here a cookie. Who likes cookies? Yeah, I love them! Let me ask you this: Is eating a cookie a sin? No, but it could be. Is it a sin if you eat a cookie that isn't yours? Yes, that is stealing. Is it a sin to eat cookies and keep eating them until you eat them all? Yes, that is gluttony. Is it a sin to eat a cookie that your mom said not to eat when you asked if you could eat a cookie? Yes, that is disobedience. Is it a sin to eat a cookie you bought at the store with your birthday money? No, that cookie belongs to you. So how do we know when it's a sin to eat a cookie and when it isn't a sin to eat a cookie? It's a sin to eat a cookie when eating the cookie means you break one of God's laws because of how you got the cookie or how many you eat. The truth is that every one of us in this room has broken one of God's laws. We have all lied or taken without permission stuff that isn't ours.

Every one of us has broken God's law, either on purpose or on accident, and there is a penalty that must be paid for breaking God's law. Just like there are punishments that happen when you break your mom and dad's rules, there are punishments that happen when we break God's law. When we break God's rules, the Bible tells us that the wages, or punishment, of sin, is death. Today in our story, we are going to look at Exodus 32, where God has just finished giving Moses his law, and Moses comes back to find the Israelites breaking the law that God just gave them!

Story:

Exodus 32:1–14, 30–35

When the people saw that Moses delayed to come down from the mountain, the people gathered themselves together to Aaron and said to him, "Up, make us gods who shall go before us. As for this Moses, the man who brought us up out of the land of Egypt, we do not know what has become of him." (v. 1)

Aaron then asked the people to give him their gold earrings and jewelry. This isn't so bad, right? He took what they handed him and made it into an idol cast in the shape of a calf, fashioning it with a tool (use a sound effect that says OH NO). Yeah, that's not good. Here is where it gets worse!

And they said, "These are your gods, O Israel, who brought you up out of the land of Egypt!" When Aaron saw this, he built an altar before it. And Aaron made a proclamation and said, "Tomorrow shall be a feast to the LORD." And they rose up early the next day and offered burnt offerings and brought peace offerings. And the people sat down to eat and drink and rose up to play. (vv. 4b–6)

God was rightly angry because of their sin. They broke a major command of God. They worshipped something other than God. Not only that, but they said, "This is the kind of god that can save us. This golden cow is what God looks like." Is that what God looks like? NO WAY.

And the LORD said to Moses, "Go down, for your people, whom you brought up out of the land of Egypt, have corrupted themselves. They have turned aside quickly out of the way that I commanded them. They have made for themselves a golden calf and have worshiped it and sacrificed to it and said, 'These are your gods, O Israel, who brought you up out of the land of Egypt!'" And the LORD said to Moses, "I have seen this people, and behold, it is a stiff-necked people. Now therefore let me alone, that my wrath may burn hot against them and I may consume them,

in order that I may make a great nation of you."
(vv. 7–10)

God said to Moses that he wanted to destroy them
because of their disobedience. Did the people of Israel sin
against God? YES! Was it right for God to want to destroy
them? YES! God always does what is right. But here is the
cool part. Moses prayed for his people.

> But Moses implored the LORD his God and said, "O
> LORD, why does your wrath burn hot against your
> people, whom you have brought out of the land of
> Egypt with great power and with a mighty hand?
> Why should the Egyptians say, 'With evil intent did
> he bring them out, to kill them in the mountains
> and to consume them from the face of the earth'?"
> (vv. 11–12a)

Did you hear that? Moses asked God to have mercy. Guess
what? He did! That's grace. God didn't destroy the people
that sinned against him. Just like he doesn't destroy us when
we put our trust in Jesus alone. We receive forgiveness and
mercy instead of destruction because we put our trust in Jesus.
Let's listen to the rest of Moses's petition. He said,

> "Turn from your burning anger and relent from this
> disaster against your people. Remember Abraham,
> Isaac, and Israel, your servants, to whom you swore
> by your own self, and said to them, 'I will multiply
> your offspring as the stars of heaven, and all this land
> that I have promised I will give to your offspring, and
> they shall inherit it forever.'" And the LORD relented
> from the disaster that he had spoken of bringing on
> his people. (vv. 12b–14)

Then Moses came down from the mountain and saw what the people were doing.

The next day Moses said to the people, "You have sinned a great sin. And now I will go up to the LORD; perhaps I can make atonement for your sin." So Moses returned to the LORD and said, "Alas, this people has sinned a great sin. They have made for themselves gods of gold. But now, if you will forgive their sin—but if not, please blot me out of your book that you have written." But the LORD said to Moses, "Whoever has sinned against me, I will blot out of my book. But now go, lead the people to the place about which I have spoken to you; behold, my angel shall go before you. Nevertheless, in the day when I visit, I will visit their sin upon them"(vv. 30–35).

Application:

Wow! We can read this story or hear this story and think to ourselves, "I can't believe they did that," or "I would never do something like that," or "What they did was really bad," or "How silly! I would never worship a golden cow." The thing that we miss in all of this is that we are just like the Israelites! Maybe we don't take a golden statue and worship it, but we do have things in our lives that we "worship" or turn to when we are afraid, alone, scared, bored, etc. This story not only shows us how bad the Israelites were, but also shows us that NONE of us can keep God's law perfectly. It shows us that we ALL sin and break God's rules, and there is a punishment or guilt that comes to us for that. Just as we saw in the story, because they broke God's law and they were unwilling, or didn't want, to repent and change, the punishment that came on the three thousand people was death.

Close:

The good news that we find hope and encouragement in today is that, even though we cannot obey God's law perfectly and we deserve the punishment of death for our sins, Jesus obeyed God's law perfectly for us. Exodus 32:30 says, "The next day Moses said to the people, 'You have sinned a great sin. And now I will go up to the Lord; perhaps I can make atonement for your sin.'"

Does anyone know what that big word "atonement" means? It means covering, and that is exactly what Jesus does for us when our faith is in him. He covers our sins so that when God looks at us, he doesn't see the sins that we commit, but he sees Jesus, who perfectly obeyed God's law and died—the punishment that we deserved. Three days later, Jesus rose from the dead, and that is the proof that God accepts Jesus's death and that we are free from the punishment of sin if we trust in Jesus. The first thing we have to do is understand and confess that we have broken God's law, on purpose and on accident. The punishment we deserve is death, and we need a Savior because we cannot save ourselves. Do you want to know what is so cool about that verse we talked about earlier? "For by grace you have been saved through faith. And this is not your own doing; it is the gift of God, not a result of works, so that no one may boast" (Ephesians 2:8–9). It shows us how we are saved—not by being good. We are saved because we belong to Christ. Our boast is the grace of God that has saved us to the uttermost.

Let's pray as we end and ask Jesus to help us. Let's confess that we are sinners in need of our perfect Savior, Jesus.

Jesus takes our guilt, covers our confessed sin with his grace, and because we are forgiven, we are filled with gratitude because Jesus has saved us. Guilt. Grace. Gratitude.

Small Groups

Activity – Team "Building"

What you need:
> *Older:*
> - 3 sheets of paper for each team
> - 3 paper clips for each team

What you do: Split kids into teams, about three to four kids per team. Give each team three sheets of paper and three paper clips. They have to work together to see who can build the tallest free-standing tower. They can't use scissors, but they can tear the paper.

What to say: Today we are going to play a "team building" game. I am going to divide you into teams and give each team three sheets of paper and three paper clips. You then will have to work together to try and build a free-standing tower from these items. You cannot use scissors, but you may tear the paper however you want. Your tower must stand for three seconds without assistance for it to qualify.

> *Younger:*
> - large cardboard blocks

What you do: Split kids into teams, about three to four kids per team. Give each team the same number of cardboard blocks. They have to work together to see who can build the tallest freestanding tower in one minute without it falling over. Play several rounds since it is quick.

What to say: Today we are going to play a team building game. I am going to divide you into teams and give you each the same number of cardboard blocks. As a team, you will work to build the tallest tower you can in one minute. Your tower will need to stand up on its own without falling to win. We will play a few times, so you can try out different ideas and see what works best!

Bring it home: Getting our towers to stand up without help was difficult. Today, in our Bible story, we learned that we can't keep God's law perfectly. We need help! Jesus came and fulfilled God's law perfectly for us. Now, because of Jesus, we don't have to try and stand up on our own. He is with us always and helps us to please God and obey God's commands.

Game - Bedsheet Ping-Pong

What you need:
- a sheet or tablecloth
- Ping-Pong ball

What you do: Players stand and hold a bedsheet on opposite ends. A Ping-Pong ball is placed onto the sheet. The sheet is then raised or lowered. The object of the game is to get the Ping-Pong ball to fall off on the other team's side of the sheet.

What to say: We are going to play a unique form of Ping-Pong. I will divide you into teams and each team will grab one side of the sheet. I will then put a Ping-Pong ball in the middle of the sheet. Each team has to raise and lower their side of the sheet to try and get the Ping-Pong ball to roll off on the other team's side. Whichever team gets to ten first wins!

Bring it home: It was hard to control which way the Ping-Pong ball went. Sometimes, it is hard for us to control our temper or our actions when we get angry. We don't realize how easily sin can creep in. Thankfully, when we put our trust in Jesus as our Savior, we know that all our sins are forgiven because he paid the price for our guilt once and for all.

Developing a Ministry Pathway

Developing a detailed ministry pathway takes work, but it's necessary work for fruitful discipleship. The sheet below provides the framework and prompts needed to brainstorm and map out your pathway. In the first section, you will write out your ministry's vision, mission, and philosophy. In the second section, you will work through potential markers or short-term goals, and in the final section, you will map out your markers on various stages of your pathway.

MINISTRY PATHWAY

How to Plan a Discipleship Strategy for Your Kids

✦ BEST MEASUREMENT ✦

📍 VISION (THE "WHY") - DESTINATION

🚗 MISSION (THE "WHAT") - VEHICLE

⊕ PHILOSOPHY (THE "WHY") - PARAMETERS

✦ PATHWAY MARKERS ✦

Long-term vision needs short-term goals

WRITE OUT MARKERS IN EACH CATEGORY

LEARN   DO   EXPERIENCE

Acknowledgments

The idea of a self-made man is a modern fallacy that damages those closest to us because it robs them of the acknowledgment that is their due, and it robs us of the humility and gratitude that deepen our understanding of the world. While there are too many to list, Hunter and I would like to thank Christ Jesus for the ability to finish such a profound personal accomplishment. It is all because of his grace we pray that all we have written will bring glory to him alone!

We also want to thank our wives, Sammie (Hunter) and Sandra (Sam). Their support, dedication, and influence have shaped our lives and these words. Thank you to our kids Margot, Clarke, Opal, and Joy (Hunter) and Gianni, Santino, Claudia, and Sabrina (Sam), who have inspired us to clarify, distill, and model what is true in all of life.

Next, we want to thank our friends and mentors who have helped us understand the beauty of Christ and his world. Your friendship has shaped our thinking and our lives. Anthony Smith, Ryan Coatney, Tim Gilley, Josh Lange, Mark Schilling, Mike Servello, Rick Andrew, Jonathan Cliff, Sean Hagarty, Brother Jim, Jared Kennedy, Matt Markins, as well as authors and theologians like Tim Keller, John Frame, Gavin Ortlund, Nate Sala, James Anderson, Jonathan Gibson, Jack Klumpenhower, Eugene Peterson, and C. S. Lewis.

Finally, thank you to the New Growth Press team: Rush Witt, Ruth Castle, Barbara Juliani, and the entire editing team for your passion and godly wisdom, which informed every decision along the way.

Endnotes

Introduction

1. Barna Research Group, *Children's Ministry in a New Reality: Building Church Communities That Cultivate Lasting Faith* (Barna Research Group, 2022), 38.

2. Barna, *Children's Ministry in a New Reality*, 39.

3. "Church Dropouts Have Risen to 64%—But What About Those Who Stay?" Barna Group, September 4, 2019, https://www.barna.com/research/resilient-disciples/.

4. "Most Teenagers Drop of Church When They Become Young Adults," Lifeway Research, January 15, 2019, https://research.lifeway.com/2019/01/15/most-teenagers-drop-out-of-church-as-young-adults/.

5. "Six Reasons Young Christians Leave Church," Barna Group, September 27, 2011, https://www.barna.com/research/six-reasons-young-christians-leave-church/.

Chapter 1

1. A. W. Tozer, "Why We Must Think Rightly About God," in *The Knowledge of the Holy* (HarperCollins, 2009), 1.

2. CRC Staff, "Counterfeit Christianity: 'Moralistic Therapeutic Deism' Most Popular Worldview in U.S. Culture," Cultural Research Center at Arizona State University, April 27, 2021, https://www.arizonachristian.edu/2021/04/27/counterfeit-christianity-moralistic-therapeutic-deism-most-popular-worldview-in-u-s-culture/.

3. C. S. Lewis, *The Chronicles of Narnia* (HarperCollins, 2001), 380.

4. Tozer, *The Knowledge of the Holy*, 4.

Chapter 2

1. Michael Patton, "What Is Theology?," Bible.org, August 22, 2005, https://bible.org/article/what-theology.

2. Reformed Theological Seminary, "About Dr. Frame," Reformed Theological Seminary, accessed June 14, 2024, https://rts.edu/people/dr-john-m-frame-emeritus/.

3. R. C. Sproul, *Knowing Scripture*, expanded ed. (InterVarsity Press, 2016), 25.

4. "Ecosystem," National Geographic, last updated March 6, 2024, https://education.nationalgeographic.org/resource/ecosystem/.

5. John M. Frame, *Systematic Theology: An Introduction to Christian Belief* (P&R Publishing, 2013), 9.

6. Scott R. Swain, "10 Things You Should Know about Systematic Theology," Crossway, October 8, 2017, https://www.crossway.org/articles/10-things-you-should-know-about-systematic-theology/.

7. Erik Raymond, "Why Must Jesus Be Both Human and Divine?," The Gospel Coalition, December 6, 2018, https://www.thegospelcoalition.org/blogs/erik-raymond/must-jesus-human-divine/.

8. Kelly M. Kapic, *A Little Book for New Theologians: Why and How to Study Theology* (InterVarsity Press, 2012), 25.

9. Howard W. Stone and James O. Duke, *How to Think Theologically*, 3rd ed. (Fortress Press, 2013).

10. American Bible Society, *State of the Bible USA 2024* (American Bible Society, 2024), 7, https://sotb.research.bible/.

11. Cambridge Advanced Learner's Dictionary, 4th ed (2013), s. v., "context."

12. "Book Overviews," Bible Project, 2024, https://bibleproject.com/explore/book-overviews/.

13. George H. Guthrie, *A Short Guide to Reading the Bible Better* (B&H Publishing Group, 2022).

14. I was reminded of this technique by my friend Adam Swing.

15. @FredFredSanders, "Every so often I get to teach the kids at church (K-5) the intro lesson before they head off to their main classes. Okay, 'every so often' means when the Trinity rolls around in our sequence of Core Concepts. Here's the 5-minute lesson I taught this time: (1/14)." Twitter post, November 22, 2021, https://twitter.com/FredFredSanders/status/1462684488408788997.

16. The Gospel Coalition, "The Simplest Way to Understand the Trinity," August 2, 2019, YouTube video, 02:53, https://www.youtube.com/watch?v=yh0sRmIb0Qk.

17. C. T. Studd, "Only One Life, Twill Soon Be Past," Reasons for Hope* Jesus, accessed April 30, 2024, https://reasonsforhopejesus.com /only-one-life-twill-soon-be-past-by-c-t-studd-1860-1931/.

Chapter 3

1. Alister McGrath, *What's the Point of Theology?: Wisdom, Well-being and Wonder* (Zondervan Academic, 2022, Kindle), Chapter 1.

2. C. S. Lewis, *The Weight of Glory* (HarperOne, 2009), 140.

3. Joshua Arnold, "Barna: Kids Will Be What They See," Family Research Council, May 5, 2022, https://www.frc.org/update article/20220505/kids-see.

4. John Tweeddale, "What Is Theology?," Reformation Bible College, October 7, 2021, https://www.reformationbiblecollege.org/ blog/what-is-theology.

5. George Barna, "American Worldview Inventory 2022 Release #5: Shocking Results Concerning the Worldview of Christian Pastors," Cultural Research Center at Arizona Christian University, May 10, 2022, https://www.arizonachristian.edu/wp-content/uploads/2022/05/ AWVI2022_Release05_Digital.pdf.

6. Paul David Tripp, *Do You Believe?: 12 Historic Doctrines to Change Your Everyday Life* (Crossway, 2021), 25.

7. McGrath, *What's the Point of Theology?*, Chapter 1.

8. Jen Pollock Michel, "Learn the Difference between Right and Almost Right," The Gospel Coalition, October 5, 2018, https://www .thegospelcoalition.org/reviews/thats-good-recovering-lost-art -discernment/. Emphasis added.

9. Barna, "American Worldview Inventory 2022 Release #5."

Chapter 4

1. Bob Smietana, "Young Bible Readers More Likely to Be Faithful Adults, Study Finds." Lifeway Research, October 17, 2017, research .lifeway.com/2017/10/17/young-bible-readers-more-likely-to-be -faithful-adults-study-finds/.

2. Eugene Peterson, *Leap Over a Wall: Earthy Spirituality for Everyday Christians* (HarperCollins, 1998), 4.

3. J. R. R. Tolkien, *Tree and Leaf* (HarperCollins, 2001), 71–72.

4. John Milton, *Paradise Lost: Authoritative Text, Sources and Backgrounds, Criticism*, ed. Gordon Teskey (W.W. Norton, 2005), 3.

5. Christopher Watkin, *Biblical Critical Theory: How the Bible's Unfolding Story Makes Sense of Modern Life and Culture* (Zondervan Academic, 2022), 59–60.

6. Watkin, *Biblical Critical Theory*, 61. The phrase—"an expression of a love always directed toward another"—is Watkin's quote from David Bentley Hart, The Beauty of the Infinite (Eerdmans, 2004).

7. George Herbert, *The Complete English Works*, Everyman's Library (Random House, 1995), 30.

8. "What Is Our Only Hope in Life and Death? | the New City Catechism." n.d. Newcitycatechism.com. Accessed June 18, 2024, https://newcitycatechism.com/new-city-catechism/#1.

9. Trevin Wax, *Gospel-Centered Teaching: Showing Christ in All the Scripture* (B&H Publishing Group, 2013), 75–83.

10. Nancy Guthrie, "Putting Together a Christ-Centered Bible Talk," The Gospel Coalition, August 5, 2021, https://www.thegospelcoalition.org/podcasts/help-me-teach-the-bible/putting-together-a-christ-centered-bible-talk/.

11. Jack Klumpenhower, *Show Them Jesus: Teaching the Gospel to Kids* (New Growth Press, 2015), 101–24.

12. Jared Kennedy, *Keeping Your Children's Ministry on Mission: Practical Strategies for Discipling the Next Generation* (Crossway, 2022, Kindle), Chapter 6.

13. Sam Luce, "Teaching the Bible's Disturbing Stories," *Sam Luce* (blog), May 3, 2018, https://samluce.com/2018/05/teaching-the-bibles-disturbing-stories/.

14. Crossway. "Since No One Can Keep the Law, What Is Its Purpose?" The New City Catechism, n.d. Accessed August 6, 2024, https://newcitycatechism.com/new-city-catechism/#15.

Chapter 5

1. Wayne Grudem, S*ystematic Theology: An Introduction to Biblical Doctrine* (Zondervan, 1994), 1183.

2. John Newton, Richard Cecil, *The Works of John Newton*, vol. 1 (Hamilton, Adams & Co., 1824), 141.

3. Eric Metaxas, *Bonhoeffer: Pastor, Martyr, Prophet, Spy* (Thomas Nelson, 2020), 64.

4. Sam Luce, "Teaching the Bible's Disturbing Stories," *Sam Luce* (blog), May 3, 2018, https://samluce.com/2018/05/teaching-the-bibles-disturbing-stories/.

Chapter 6

1. Sydney Shea, "Over 70% of Young Democrats Wouldn't Date Republicans: Poll," *Washington Examiner*, December 9, 2021,

https://www.washingtonexaminer.com/politics/over-70-of-young
-democrats-wouldnt-date-republicans-poll.

2. Chris Palusky, "Christians, let's stop fighting each other and
serve our neighbors in need instead," *USA Today*, June 29, 2021,
https://www.usatoday.com/story/opinion/voices/2021/06/29/american
-christians-turning-people-off-church-bethany-christian-services
/5370555001/.

3. James K. A. Smith, *You Are What You Love: The Spiritual Power
of Habit* (Brazos Press, 2016), 7.

4. Kyle Borg, "What Is Charity?" Ligonier Ministries, March 3,
2023, https://www.ligonier.org/learn/articles/virtues-vices-charity.

5. Michael Horton, *The Christian Faith: A Systematic Theology for
Pilgrims on the Way* (Zondervan, 2011), 267.

6. Blaise Pascal, *Pensées*, trans. A. J. Krailsheimer (E. P. Dutton,
1958), 161.

7. G. K. Chesterton, *Heretics—Classic Illustrated Edition* (John
Lane Co., 1905), 159.

8. Chesterton, *Heretics*, 158.

9. Gavin Ortlund, *Finding the Right Hills to Die On: The Case for
Theological Triage* (Crossway, 2020), 96.

10. Saint Augustine, *On Christian Doctrine: Theological Treatise on
the Teachings of Scriptures* (e-artnow, 2021, Kindle), Chapter 27.

11. Paul J. Wadell, "Charity: How Friendship with God Unfolds
in Love for Others," in *Virtues and Their Vices*, ed. Kevin Timpe and
Craig A. Boyd (Oxford Academic, 2014), https://academic.oup.com/
book/2925/chapter-abstract/143586124?redirectedFrom=fulltext.

Chapter 7

1. "Our Mission" and "Our Vision," Awana, accessed April 30,
2024, https://www.awana.org/leadershipdevelopment/wp-content/
uploads/sites/8/2018/04/Awana_mission-vision.pdf.

2. Ryan Coatney and Hunter Williams, "The BEST Way to
Teach Kids Is…," August 29, 2023, in *Cross Formed Kidmin*, podcast,
https://podcasts.apple.com/us/podcast/cross-formed-kidmin/id167
1646993?i=1000626041092.

3. Eugene H. Peterson, *A Long Obedience in the Same Direction:
Discipleship in an Instant Society* (InterVarsity Press, 2021), 160.

4. Joe Carter, "10 Things You Should Know About Catechesis,"
Crossway, April 17, 2017, https://www.crossway.org/articles/10-things
you-should-know-about-catechesis/.

5. Timothy Keller, "Why Catechesis Now?," *Timothy Keller* (blog), October 11, 2012, https://timothykeller.com/blog/2012/10/11/why-catechesis-now.

6. Timothy Keller, *The New City Catechism: 52 Questions and Answers for Our Hearts and Minds* (Crossway, 2017).

7. Kevin Hippolyte, Jared Kennedy, and Trey Kullman, *Faith Builder Catechism: Devotions to Level Up Your Family Discipleship* (New Growth Press, 2023).

8. Starr Meade, *Comforting Hearts, Teaching Minds: Family Devotions Based on the Heidelberg Catechism* (P&R Books, 2013).

9. Starr Meade, *Training Hearts, Teaching Minds: Family Devotions Based on the Shorter Catechism* (P&R Books, 2000).

10. Ryan Coatney and Hunter Williams, "Catechisms: The Game Changer for Your Children's Ministry," July 10, 2023, in *Cross Formed Kidmin*, podcast, https://crossformedkids.com/022-catechisms-the-game-changer-for-your-childrens-ministry/.

11. Katarina von Schlegel, "Be Still, My Soul; The Lord Is on Thy Side," Hymnary, accessed August 13, 2024, https://hymnary.org/text/be_still_my_soul_the_lord_is_on_thy_side.

12. "About the Gospel Story Hymnal," Word & Wonder, accessed August 13, 2024, https://wordandwonder.org/about/hymnal/.

13. Keith and Kristyn Getty, *Getty Kids Hymnal* (Getty Music, 2021).

Chapter 8

1. Barna Research Group, *Children's Ministry in a New Reality: Building Church Communities That Cultivate Lasting Faith* (Barna Research Group, 2022), 33–36.

2. Imed Bouchrika, "101 American School Statistics: 2024 Data, Trends & Predictions," Research.com, July 16, 2024, https://research.com/education/american-school-statistics.

3. Christian Smith and Amy Adamczyk, *Handing Down the Faith: How Parents Pass Their Religion on to the Next Generation* (Oxford University Press, 2021), 69.

4. Matt Adair, "Gospel-Centered Leadership—Transparency," Gospel-Centered Discipleship, May 18, 2012, https://gcdiscipleship.com/pre2019-articles/2012/05/18/gospel-centered-leadership-transparency?rq=Gospel-Centered%20Leadership%20Transparency.

5. Smith and Adamczyk, *Handing Down the Faith*, 72.

Conclusion

1. C. S. Lewis, *The Chronicles of Narnia Complete 7-Book Collection* (HarperCollins, 2013), 801.

Appendix 1

1. Trevin Wax, *Gospel-Centered Teaching: Showing Christ in All the Scripture* (B&H Publishing Group, 2013), 75–83.

2. Nancy Guthrie, "Putting Together a Christ-Centered Bible Talk," The Gospel Coalition, August 5, 2021, https://www.thegospel coalition.org/podcasts/help-me-teach-the-bible/putting-together -a-christ-centered-bible-talk/.

3. Jared Kennedy, *Keeping Your Children's Ministry on Mission: Practical Strategies for Discipling the Next Generation* (Crossway, 2022, Kindle), Chapter 5.

4. Kennedy, *Keeping Your Children's Ministry on Mission*, Chapter 5.

Appendix 2

1. Wayne Grudem, *Systematic Theology: An Introduction to Biblical Doctrine* (Zondervan, 1994), 1183.